The Essential Gluten-Baking Guide

PART 2 Learn how to use Sweet Rice, Sorghum, Buckwheat, Teff, Cassava and Potato Flour in 50+ recipes

TriumphDining

Brittany Angell
Iris Higgins

The Essential Gluten-Free Baking Guide Part 2
by Brittany Angell & Iris Higgins

Copyright ©2012 by Triumph Dining
http://www.triumphdining.com

ISBN 978-1-938104-01-5

Book cover design by Jeff Weeks
Photos by Matt Calabrese, Calabrese Studios
Interior design and layout by Val Sherer, Personalized Publishing Services

Triumph Dining
144 Diablo Ranch Court, Danville, CA 94506 USA

Table of Contents

Acknowledgments

This book would not have been possible without a number of people and companies. We give our heartfelt thanks to:

JK Gourmet, Honeyville Grains, Dakota Prairie, Nuts.com, Big Tree Farms, Simply Organic, Navitas Naturals, Shiloh Farms and Garden of Life .

Photography: Matt Calabrese

Videography: Bruce Begy

Researchers: Ashley Ayres, Season Fagan

Recipe Formatting: Alexis Mettler

Baking Assistant: Maia A'Brams Horvath

Recipe Testers: Christine Holzmann, Jessica L. Angell, Laurel VanBlarcum, Gina Pagano, Sherman Sherman, Linda Stiles, Betsy Higgins, Alta Mantsch, Kim Boggs, Deanna Schneider, Julia Simpson, Sarah Stivers, Angela Kuhn, Suzanne Hill, Lindsay Keach, Georgianna Reilly, Jessica Rodgers, Ginger Garza, Noelle Rose, Ricki Heller, Julia Berger, Laura King, Erica Nafziger, Amanda Hockham, Ande Baker, Deborah Baca-Dietz, Emily Smith, Tessa Thralls, Abby Pattison, Tre Gallery, Rose Myers, Rebecca Haacke, Jen Repard, Abbie Brown, Christine Nygren, Maggie Savage, Heather Graffam, Debi Smith, Teresa Wright, Alexa Croft, Jennifer Brunett, Katrina Morales, Alea Milham, Stephanie Laidlaw, Brooke Lippy, Zoe Hastings, Olivia Davis, Diane Eblin, Kalinda Piper, Heather Riley, Lisa Chalfant, Elizabeth Howes, Anney Ryan, Adriane Angarano, Amy Fratto, Jillian Punska, Heidi Kelly, Beverly Lane, Terri Tremblett, Krista Brouwer, Kristin Batson, Amy Harms Munson, Tina Pruett, Jey Rodgers, Dana Hantel, Jenni Schneider, Sherry Varano, Dr. Jennifer Feather, Kris Weimer, Kaitlyn Renfrow, Selene Nemethy-Fekete, Crystal Braylor

This book was a labor of love that was made with so many helping hands. Brittany, you are an amazing and devoted baker. Thank you, Rich, for keeping Brittany sane, and for your late night edits and countless taste tests. Thank you Dave Morris and Triumph Dining for giving us the creative freedom to make this book.

My family, I love you and credit you all for making me the person I am. Ladies of the Kenmore Estate, past and present, thank you for giving up your kitchen, for countless taste testings, and for your support. Lily, Hayley, my Tufts crew, and Micaela and Sarah, thank you for supporting my dreams and cheering me on. Steve, The Daily Dietribe would not exist without you. The Krivicich Family, your love and support has meant more than you will ever know. Emareya and Steven, you bring me peace. Bastyr community, my professors, Doris, the wonderful staff: thank you for supporting this endeavor! All my teachers, from pre-school on, thank you for getting me to this point and teaching me so much!

To Calder, for giving me the freedom to follow my dreams, and for following yours.

Iris Higgins

The past few years of my life have been a whirlwind of gifts of kindness. The following people helped to propel the dream that was this book into reality:

Iris Higgins, you are a true friend and confidant, a woman with an incredible work ethic and dedication. You inspired me, challenged me to work harder, and questioned me when others might be too afraid to do so. Thank you for your continual support, encouragement and honesty. I could not have asked for a better partner in crime!

Jason Berardi, you placed into my life a platform that allowed me to dance. John Maggio led me to Triumph Dining via Pam Sherman.

Dave Morris and Triumph Dining, thank you for taking a chance on me.

Don and Julie Riling, my parents, have provided me with their love and a confidence in spite of my stubborn nature. Brenton Riling, my brother, I appreciate all the help you have given me with Real Sustenance.

My husband, Rich Angell, has provided humor and willingness to taste every single item our oven produced. You have been my rock through my dramatic ups and downs over the many failures and successful baking quests. You encourage me and keep me humble.

Clyde and Chloe, my beloved rat terriers, you are a constant source of happiness and my daily companions in the kitchen!

Brittany Angell

Foreword

· · · · · · · · · · · · · · · · · · ·

In the world of gluten-free baking I am often the teacher. But today I am the student, learning new things about gluten-free baking and flours from Brittany Angell and Iris Higgins. In fact, there's something for every gluten-free baker in their book, *The Essential Gluten-Free Baking Guide.* These newcomers to the gluten-free scene have done their homework, helping to simplify gluten-free baking and introducing us to new flours. Not only does the book feature the gluten-free flours, one chapter at a time and in more than 50 recipes, it also includes commentary and tips from veteran bakers. This book is a resource that every gluten-free baker should have in their kitchen.

One size does not fit all when it comes to creating gluten-free recipes. It takes a pantry full of flours and gums to create something that tastes good and has great texture. And the more choices we have, the better our baking will be. This primer presents an in-depth look at each flour and its role in gluten-free baking. The book is rich in detail with chapters like "Understanding White and Brown Rice Flour" and "Understanding the Starches," as well as discussions about weight versus volume and replacing xanthan gum in recipes.

This book also offers tips on substituting flours, baking without eggs, corn, soy, dairy, replacing refined sugar with sugar alternatives, and creating your own recipes. One of my favorites is the section on yeast breads. Can one have too many great bread recipes? I think not.

As someone who was diagnosed with celiac disease 35 years ago, a time when there were no resources available, I marvel at how far gluten-free baking has come. I went to culinary school to learn how recipes were constructed then taught myself to make them over so they were safe for my diet. Back then my choices were rice flour and soy flour. I never dreamed of blending flours or using starches, and xanthan and guar gum did not exist. It never occurred to me to improve upon the gritty foods that fell apart the moment I took a bite. I wish I had had books like this one back then.

The day I created my first gluten-free yeast bread with a blend of flours and gum and produced a loaf that rose and domed and tasted like real bread, I nearly fainted. That masterful recipe propelled me into a new era and I began creating blends and making mixes for others. I thought, "After all, wouldn't every other gluten-free person want these wonderful treats?"

Indeed they did. It was the beginning of the line of Gluten-Free Pantry baking mixes, blends that provided people with gourmet treats that held together and tasted great.

Year after year, gluten-free baking has become more sophisticated. Healthy flours have joined the line-up, producing products that are nutritional and filled with fiber. And, with it, folks tell me, "I wish I knew how to use amaranth, or quinoa or buckwheat or sorghum."

The answers are all here in The Essential Gluten-Free Baking Guide. Brittany and Iris are natural teachers. The pair have created a go-to resource for gluten- and wheat-free bakers. These books will have a place of honor on my shelf of favorite cookbooks.

Beth Hillson, Gluten-Free Makeovers, Living Without Magazine

Introduction

· ·

I want to tell you a little story. In the early 2000s I went to a birthday party for a friend who had celiac disease. I didn't fully understand what that meant, but I did know that he couldn't eat the same things I could. Wanting to do something special for him, I went to the store and bought a bag of Bob's Red Mill White Rice Flour. I took my favorite recipe for lemon bars and made them, substituting the flours. The result wasn't awful, but it certainly wouldn't have impressed anyone. At that time I had no idea that there were more than a dozen different types of gluten-free flours. I had never heard of tapioca or potato starch, and I certainly didn't know what arrowroot starch was. Xanthan gum wasn't even on my radar screen, and using it to keep baked goods from crumbling? I didn't even know gluten-free baked goods had a crumbling problem!

I was clueless.

Fast-forward a couple of years. A lifelong struggle with digestive issues spiraled out of control. I found myself falling asleep all the time, had a headache that never went away, and was generally depressed. My doctors were stumped. Encouraged by the recipient of the gluten-free lemon bars, I stopped eating gluten. And just like that my life changed. I woke up the next day feeling better than I had in months and jumped wholeheartedly into the gluten-free lifestyle. Surely my friends and family got tired of hearing me talk about it, but I wanted to shout it to the rooftops. Being gluten-free was the best thing that had ever happened to me.

At first it was just about learning what foods I couldn't tolerate, navigating restaurants, and learning how to be my own health advocate. Eventually, though, I wanted something else: I wanted to make lemon bars that were just as good as the ones I ate in childhood. During this process, I had started a blog called The Daily Dietribe (www.thedailydietribe.com), and I started to share the recipes I was creating. My hobby quickly turned into an obsession. I developed a love for baking I never had when I was eating gluten because gluten-free baking was such a challenge and there were so many different flours to play with. I loved the challenge of making over a recipe to be gluten-free.

Facebook led me to a friendship with blogger Brittany Angell. A conversation we had about coconut flour sparked more talk over how to use the different flours. From opposite sides of the country our minds began to whirl and pretty soon we had decided: we were going to make it our mission to understand how all the gluten-free flours worked and to share that information with other confused bakers out there.

The *Essential Gluten-Free Baking Guides* are a compendium of everything Brittany and I have learned about gluten-free flours. Once this idea was firmly in place, we worked non-stop to develop recipes that we know you'll love! In some cases, we've tested a recipe with all 12 flours just to see how each one worked. We've tried out various techniques and given our recipes to over seventy different testers. We've researched and laughed and cried. We've thrown failed loaves of bread on the floor in disgust. And we've learned more than I ever thought I would know, not just about gluten-free baking, but about the chemistry of baking in general, about the time and effort that goes into writing a cookbook, and about the people that we wrote these guides for. This book is for you. This book is about more than recipes. It's about giving you the confidence that you can bake anything you want, no matter what your dietary needs are. We don't ever want you to look at something with longing and think, "I can't eat that." Brittany and I think about how we can make things and we are going to teach you to do it as well.

Oh, and in case you were wondering, I did make those lemon bars again, and you'll find the recipe here in our sweet white rice flour chapter. I have a feeling my friend will like these ones a lot better.

Iris Higgins

Chapter 1

How to Use This Book

We developed *The Essential Guides* to help you understand how each of the gluten-free flours work. Our goal was to help you get a handle on the flavor, texture and weight attributes that the flours give to baked goods. There are numerous gluten-free flours on the market, and usually a dozen can be found in your local grocery store. We selected a group that we felt were the most accessible and dedicated each chapter of these guides to a different flour. Our recipes have been formatted in the following way:

- Each recipe has been limited to the use of the featured flour, rice flour and the starches (tapioca, arrowroot or potato starch). The rice flour and starches play a background role in these recipes and allow the featured flour to show off its best qualities. For those looking to avoid rice flour refer to to page 14 for our suggested substitutions.

- We recommend preparing several recipes from each chapter to get a handle on the flour's taste and texture. Tasting the different flours in the recipes is important to the learning process. Plus, we have a hunch that you really might enjoy eating it all because it tastes so good!

- To keep things simple, our ingredients lists call for butter and milk. However, you can feel confident that we tested all of our recipes with dairy-free ingredients as well. When a recipe calls for butter, we have also tested it with Earth Balance Soy-Free Buttery Spread. When a recipe calls for milk, we have tested it with a variety of dairy-free milks, including almond, hemp and soy milk. For more information on replacing dairy, see our dairy section later in this chapter.

- Buy a scale and use the gram measurements to achieve best results. If you choose to use measuring cups, our measurements will either say *lightly filled cup* or *packed cup*. Lightly filled means you should scoop flour into your measuring cup and then level it off with a knife. Packed means you can scoop your measuring cup straight into the bag of flour. For starches and ingredients such as cornmeal, it doesn't matter if you scoop or pack, you'll get approximately the same results either way.

- If a recipe specifies that an ingredient should be room temperature or chilled, make sure to follow that direction. Having an ingredient at the wrong temperature can mean the difference between a beautifully risen loaf of bread or a dense loaf with a collapsed crust.

- To achieve our results, it is imperative that you use only the ingredients that we specify, at least the first time you make it; you can experiment after that. Avoid assumptions that the ingredients you have on hand will give you positive results. For example: superfine rice flour gives entirely different results than regular rice flour.

- When our recipes specify unrefined granulated sugar, we have tested them with Sucanat, turbinado cane sugar, coconut palm sugar, and xylitol.

- Everyone likes to experiment. We suggest any changes to recipes be made one at a time. Any change can drastically affect a recipe and if your change creates a flop you can easily backtrack to find out where you went wrong.

- Many of our recipes use double acting baking powder; it gives the best overall results. If you can't find it in your local store then order some from Bobsredmill.com. If this is not an option, regular baking powder will work but your baked good will lack some rise.

- A quick note on storing flours. White rice flour and starches can be stored at room temperature. Store all other flours in the fridge or freezer to prevent rancidity.

- Baking is a science. Changes to any recipe will affect the outcome. If you do choose to make changes be sure to take notes! Don't be afraid of experimentation! There are no failed recipes, only opportunities to learn.

When to Use All-Purpose Mixes in Our Recipes

We haven't tested every recipe here with all-purpose mixes and cannot guarantee successful results. That said, pancakes, waffles, muffins and quick breads typically work well using all-purpose flour mixes. You can make substitutions by adding up the total cups of flour and starch in the recipe and replacing them with an equal amount (in cups) of your favorite all-purpose mix. We do not recommend using an all-purpose flour mix for any of our recipes containing almond flour, coconut flour, sweet rice flour, potato flour or cassava.

Understanding Baking Soda and Baking Powder

Baking soda and powder are both made from baking soda. Baking soda is a chemical leavener that must come into contact with an acid (such as buttermilk, lemon juice or vinegar) to generate the reaction needed to produce carbon dioxide. The carbon dioxide creates the rise we so desire from our gluten-free baked goods. However, not all recipes contain these acids, which is why some recipes require baking powder. Baking powder is baking soda combined with an acid and cornstarch. The cornstarch keeps the two ingredients dry and non-reactive until they are introduced to moisture.

You'll notice that some recipes require both baking soda and powder because the use of both guarantees that the baked good will rise. Some recipes call for baking soda, baking powder and an acid. Why? The reaction from the baking soda and vinegar occurs quickly in the baking process. However, the

baking soda eventually neutralizes the acids. Upon this neutralization, the baking powder kicks in to provide the rest of the "lift". Think of those volcanoes you made as a child. The initial burst of foam from the vinegar and baking soda quickly fizzled out. To keep the experiment going you had to add more. The same concept occurs in the oven. If you are combining baking soda and an acid in a recipe, it's important to move the baked good into the oven as quickly as possible after mixing. Many of our recipes use double acting baking powder to better guarantee that this added boost occurs in the oven.

Understanding White and Brown Rice Flour

It would be convenient to use a single flour to achieve perfect recipes. Unfortunately gluten-free baking simply doesn't work that way. A few flours can be used on their own but most often another flour or starch will need to be added for proper results.

Brown rice flour and white rice flour work similarly, but white rice flour is lower in fi-

ber and other nutrients. Brown rice flour will make your recipes taste just a bit heartier, which is why we like to use white rice flour in recipes that we want to be especially fluffy or delicate.

Recommended Brands:
- **Nuts.com**
- **Bobsredmill**

If you must avoid rice flour for allergy reasons we suggest you replace it with sorghum flour or millet flour for the most comparable results.

Superfine Rice Flour

This phenomenal flour goes into its own category. There is a huge difference between regular rice and superfine rice flour. The difference is in the milling process in which the grain is ground into flour. Superfine is far superior in quality as it has been finely ground. This superfine flour has many benefits in baking. It absorbs more liquid, and gives baked goods great texture and a better rise. A number of our recipes were designed to use superfine rice flour. It is absolutely essential that it is used in these instances; neglecting to do so will give you poor results.

Both brown and white rice flour can be purchased superfine. We did extensive testing with a number of brands and discovered that several companies do an exceptional job milling their flours. We noticed they had superfine qualities without being called superfine. Dakota Prairie rice flours fall into this category. Their brown and white rice flour worked wonderfully in all of our super-

fine applications. Therefore, we placed their brand into the superfine category.

The rice flour found at your neighborhood Asian grocery store also falls into the unlabeled superfine category. These are a terrific and inexpensive alternative (approximately $1 per pound) to some of the other flours. We use this flour cup for cup in place of superfine with perfect results every time.

Recommended Brands:
- **Authentic Foods Superfine (brown or white)**
- **Dakota Prairie (brown or white)** *Note:* **not titled superfine**
- **Rice Flour from Asian grocery stores**

Many gluten-free baked goods using rice flour have the tendency to lose their soft texture when they become cold. This can be solved by re-heating the baked good prior to serving.

Understanding the Starches: Tapioca, Potato, Arrowroot, and Cornstarch

Starches help lighten recipes and bind ingredients together. For the most part, the starches can be exchanged gram for gram or cup for cup. They each impart a slightly different texture and flavor. We often like to use a mix of tapioca and potato starch.

Tapioca Starch: Tends to make recipes like cookies both crispy and chewy. Using too much tapioca starch in your recipes can result in a gummy texture.

Potato Starch: Makes recipes a little lighter and fluffier than tapioca starch. We use it with breads and pancakes for extra lift. We've also found that potato starch soaks up more liquid in recipes than the other starches. We like to use it for crispy baked goods such as crackers.

Arrowroot Starch: Very similar to and can be substituted for tapioca starch. Arrowroot is not included in any of our recipes in this book for one reason: cost. Tapioca is much less expensive and equally as effective.

Cornstarch: Won't be found in our recipes for one word: corn. Corn allergies are widespread. In many recipes, cornstarch can be exchanged for tapioca or arrowroot starch.

Most people develop a preference for a starch they like best. We encourage you to experiment to discover your own starch preference.

The Great Debate Cups (Volume) vs. Grams

Is the investment in a good quality scale worth it?

When you measure a cup of flour three times, you'll likely come out with three different numbers. Sometimes those measurements only differ by a few grams. Other times, they're off by 20 or 30 grams. We've had recipes work perfectly for one tester and fail for another because they measured their flours differently. With grams, you can be sure you're following our recipes exactly. We encourage you to closely follow the weight measurements in our recipes or you may get varied results. Plus, if you measure by weight, you cut down on dishes to wash because you simply measure all of your ingredients straight into one bowl.

If weight is so important then why do we include volume measurements? It's because we both use volume in our own baking. We keep track of our weight measurements so that we can reproduce recipes exactly from one time to the next. But when we're substituting one flour for another, we have found volume measurements work better for us. We know this is different from what most people will tell you, so let us explain.

In our research, we kept reading that in substituting one flour for another, you had to do it by weight, not volume. Yet in our own baking, we subbed by volume and never had a problem. Feeling confused by this, Iris decided to do a little experiment. She took our

Sesame Buckwheat Breakfast Cookie recipe and played around with substitutions. She replaced the buckwheat with an equal volume of sorghum flour. Then she made the cookies again, replacing the buckwheat with an equal weight of sorghum flour. She did this with various individual flours, and also with Bob's Red Mill All-Purpose Mix. The results were the same every time. When she subbed in another flour by volume, the resulting cookie came out similarly to the original. When she subbed in another flour by weight, the batter was thinner and the cookie spread too much. This is counter to what we've always read. To confuse matters even more, she found the results were the opposite when subbing potato starch for tapioca starch. With the starches, it seemed, the cookies worked better when subbing by weight, not volume, although the difference is negligible either way.

Here's what we believe. Conventional wisdom will tell you to substitute one flour for another by weight. What we've found in our kitchens is that you should only sub the starches by weight. Flours should be subbed by volume and so should all-purpose mixes. You should test this out in your own kitchen and see what *you* find! Take a favorite recipe and sub in a different flour by weight. Then sub in that same flour by volume, and see which recipe turns out better. We know what happened in our kitchens. We'd love to know what happens in yours.

Recommended Brands:
- **OXO**
- **Escali**

How to convert a recipe to gluten-free:

If you do an Internet search, you'll find a variety of suggestions. We've learned that each baker has his or her own way of starting this process. We like to do one of two things. Either:

Make your own gluten-free flour blend (directions on how to do this to follow) or use an all-purpose flour blend to start, add ½ teaspoon xanthan gum per cup of flour, and substitute it cup for cup with wheat flour. Once you see how that turns out, you can begin making changes based on your results.

or

Almost everything you could want gluten-free has been made by someone already. Find a recipe from a source you trust, and start with that. Then make substitutions based on your desired ingredients, texture and flavor.

How to make a gluten-free flour blend:

Sift together:
1 cup flour (any flour you like) +
1 cup flour (any other flour you like) +
1 cup starch (your preference of starch)
_____

3 cups all-purpose mix

You can use any two types of flour (except almond, cassava or potato flour) for this.

How to make gluten-free yeast breads:

Gluten-free yeast breads are the most challenging aspect of gluten-free baking. Who hasn't heard horror stories about gluten-free bread that turned out as hard as a doorstop? This challenge scared us more than any other in this project but we were determined to conquer it. After hundreds of trials and a few headaches, we finally understand the basics of gluten-free yeast bread. There are a number of yeasted bread recipes in these guides that you will love.

Here are some of our tips:

- Gluten-free yeast breads are not like yeast breads made with gluten. One difference is the kneading process. There are very few gluten-free recipes that will call for kneading. Generally we prefer to use a hand or stand mixer to do the kneading for us.

- Gluten-free breads only need to rise once whereas wheat-based breads need to rise several times. Thus, the preparation for gluten-free yeast breads takes less time.

- Xanthan gum and gum replacements like whole psyllium husks are very important in creating structure in bread recipes. In a round of experimentation for our Artisan Sandwich Bread, we tried using ¼ teaspoon less of xanthan gum and our bread lost 4 full inches of height!

- Focus on the protein. Protein gives yeast breads the structure they require. We had great success when we combined a bean flour with superfine rice flour and potato starch. Other high protein flours can yield great results as well.

- Eggs are a gluten-free bread's best friend. We like to beat our eggs heavily in our recipes to add some extra volume. We also like to add stiff egg whites to our bread batters.

- Superfine flours are recommended for gluten-free bread because they help the bread poof up higher. These superfine flours have a smaller grain size and therefore are lighter in weight. This allows the yeast to spring up. Heavy grainy flours weigh the loaf down.

- Gluten-free yeast breads require more liquid. If there's not enough liquid, the flour will weigh the dough down and it will not rise. Too much liquid will cause your bread to rise too much. It will become a "poufy bread monster" with giant air pockets and it may also collapse.

- In most cases gluten-free breads need to be made in a pan to give them the proper shape. Since their batter is runny, they will spread rather than rise without the support.

- Gluten-filled recipes rise easily. You stick them on the stove and they just grow. This is not always the case with gluten-free. We give our gluten-free breads a fighting chance to rise by using specific proofing methods. Proofing the dough in a warm moist location makes all the difference in the world. Here are our favorite methods:

Best Methods for Proofing Your Dough

(*a.k.a.* **how to make a steam box**):

1. Our #1 method for getting your dough to rise is to make a steam box in your microwave. Put two microwave-safe jars filled with water in the microwave and turn it on for about 15-20 minutes. Prepare bread dough while you wait. When the dough is ready to rise, quickly open the microwave and stick your bowl of dough inside. Shut it quickly so the steam doesn't escape. Let rise for the duration as per the instructions. *Note:* Opening the microwave door to check on the bread causes the needed steam to escape. Don't let your curiosity get the best of you!

2. If you don't have a microwave or your recipe calls for the dough to be shaped before rising (such as with our Soft Pretzels recipe), make a steam box in your oven. Turn the oven on to the lowest heat. Then put an oven-safe bowl of water on the lowest rung. Once the oven is pre-heated, turn it off to cool while you prepare your dough. Once the dough is ready to rise, place a towel over it and place it into the oven. Allow the bread to rise for the required time.

3. A third method that works surprisingly well is the stove-top method. Put your dough into a large skillet. Put the top on the skillet and turn the burner on low for 2 minutes. Then turn it off and let the dough rise. This method traps condensation in the pan. We use this method for our English Muffins, Cheesy Skillet Biscuits and Cilantro Pesto Stuffed Rolls.

Understanding Alternative Sweeteners

Sugar is more than a sweetener when used in baked goods. It's an important ingredient that provides moisture, structure and browning when baked. There are many types of sweeteners on the market today. They come in two forms: liquid and granulated. Liquid sweeteners are, as their name implies, liquid in nature. Granulated sugars are crystallized. Many people like to substitute sugars in their recipes. It's fine to substitute, but keep in mind the texture and flavor you are trying to achieve. These will change with any substitutions. The more you experiment the better you'll understand the behavior of each sweetener.

There are a vast number of options for both liquid and granulated sweeteners. These different sugars come in a variety of price points and each offer their own health benefits. For this book we chose to use primarily the unrefined healthier varieties. One of the most common questions we are asked is how these different sugars can be exchanged in baked good recipes. It's not an easy question to answer but we've spent months experimenting and what follows are our discoveries:

Granulated Sugars
Organic Cane Sugar

White cane sugar and organic cane sugar are generally the same. The glycemic index is lower in organic cane sugar and it tends to be coarser.

We have successfully replaced them cup for cup. Most of our recipes call for the use of unrefined granulated sugar. In most of these recipes regular inexpensive table sugar will work, unless otherwise specified.

Recommended Brand:
- **Woodstock Farms Pure Cane Sugar**

Turbinado *a.k.a.* Raw Sugar:

Turbinado sugar is made from cane juice, just like sugar. It is extracted during an earlier period in the processing and retains some of the nutrients and flavor of molasses. Turbinado sugar can be used as a substitute for brown or white sugar

Pros: Many claim that turbinado sugar is healthier because it's less processed, is lower in calories than granulated sugar and contains trace amount of minerals.

Cons: Turbinado sugar undergoes processing to produce the finished product and loses most of its molasses and nutrient content. While it is lower on the glycemic index than refined table sugar, turbinado sugar does raise your blood sugar so we don't recommend it for diabetics.

Baking Tips:
- This sugar is usually very coarsely ground and is perfect sprinkled on top of baked goods or rolled into cookies.

- This coarse grind can be problematic in baked goods as it will take longer to break down in the oven. You can run the sugar through a coffee grinder or process it in your blender to create a powder. This will give your baked goods a better overall texture and allow for the sugar to do its job.

- It works well as a replacement for white granulated sugar cup for cup when it is powdered.
- It will add a very light golden color to baked goods.

Sucanat:

Sucanat is pure dried sugar cane juice. Through a mechanical process of heating and cooling the juice, small sugar grains are formed. Sucanat is generally accepted as a substitute for brown sugar.

Pros: It contains trace amount of nutrients as it is not as highly processed as white sugar. It can be used as a 1:1 replacement for refined sugar.

Cons: Although less refined, it's still sugar and is problematic for people with certain health problems, such as diabetes.

Baking Tips:

- This sugar works wonderfully as a replacement for brown sugar because of its caramel flavor. However, it contains less moisture than brown sugar since brown sugar contains molasses. To replicate brown sugar we suggest adding some molasses to your Sucanat in recipes.
- Will lend baked goods a light brown/dark golden color.
- Like many other sugars, it is coarsely ground. Please read recipe instructions carefully. Some may require you

to powder the unrefined granulated sugar. If you don't, results will vary.

- Makes wonderful frosting and glazes in powdered form.
- Palm sugar can be replaced with Sucanat cup for cup, yielding extremely similar results. They provide a similar flavor and moisture level to baked goods.
- Can be used as a cup for cup replacement for white sugar in most applications. That being said, you will notice that Sucanat will add less moisture to your baked goods than regular white sugar. Exchanging the two sugars may be problematic in recipes with a sensitive moisture content (e.g. graham crackers, biscotti or fried doughnuts).

Recommended Brand:

- **Wholesome Sweeteners Organic Sucanat**

Coconut Palm Sugar:

Coconut palm sugar is made from the sap of the coconut tree. The taste is similar to brown sugar, with a sweet hint of molasses.

Pros: Coconut palm sugar has a low glycemic index. This makes it a safer choice for diabetics or anyone looking to watch their weight. It is rich in many vitamins and minerals.

Cons: Coconut palm sugar can be expensive and is not as widely available as other sweeteners.

Baking Tips

- Palm sugar works the same as Sucanat. Refer to the tips on Sucanat for how to use it.

Recommended Brands:

- **Navitas Naturals**
- **Big Tree Farms: In addition to regular coconut palm sugar, Big Tree Farms has palm sugar that has been infused with other flavors: ginger, turmeric, and vanilla. These are good additions to both sweet and savory baked goods.**

Maple Sugar:

As the name implies, maple sugar is made from the syrup that comes from maple trees. Often made into tasty maple candy, it can also be turned into a sugar for baking.

Pros: This is often considered a more natural choice than sugar. It is sweeter than sugar, thus less will be needed in baking applications.

Cons: It is high on the glycemic index and is expensive and difficult to find.

Baking Tips:

- Substitute ⅔ cup of maple sugar for every 1 cup of granulated sugar in your recipes.

- Wonderful for streusel toppings.

Recommended Brand:

- **Shiloh Farms**

Date Sugar:

Date sugar is a natural sweetener produced by powdering or grinding dehydrated dates. It is light brown in color, has a very sweet taste, and a grainy texture.

Pros: Can be used in baking where the recipe does not require melting of sugar. One cup of refined sugar can be replaced by about two-thirds cup of date sugar. It's a better source of vitamins and minerals than refined table sugar.

Cons: Dates are high on the glycemic index, and are not recommended for diabetics.

Baking Tips:

- Use in a 1:1 ratio for granulated sugar.

- Delicious sweetener to use in raw recipes, like raw cheesecakes.

- Can be used to create a crunchy texture when rolled into cookies.

- Run this sugar through your coffee grinder or in your blender to create a finely ground powdered sugar. It will work great in frosting recipes.

- Date sugar will add a brown tint to the applications where it is added.

Recommended Brand:

- **Shiloh Farms**

Stevia:

Stevia extract comes from the plant of the same name, also known as stevia rebaudiana. You can grow the plant just as you would any other herb and mince it for use in cooking or teas.

Pros: Stevia does not raise blood sugar and has zero calories. It is a suitable option for diabetics or anyone watching their weight or blood sugar.

Cons: Many brands of stevia have a strong aftertaste and it is expensive. However, a little goes a long way so your bottle will last for a long time. We chose not to use stevia recipes in this book because it is an acquired taste and many people do not like it. However, we both use stevia and you can find stevia-sweetened recipes on our blogs.

Baking Tips:

Note that when we talk about baking with stevia, we're talking about the liquid or crystal extracts that are made up only of stevia. You can buy stevia products that have fillers in them to make it easier to use cup for cup as a substitute for sugar.

- Stevia cannot be used cup for cup in baked good recipes.

- Stevia is especially effective when used in conjunction with small amounts of honey or other natural sugars. It increases their sweetness exponentially so that less sugar may be used in a recipe.

- A little bit goes a long way. Using too much will create an unappealing aftertaste.

- About ⅓-½ teaspoon of powdered stevia (depending on the brand) = 1 cup of sugar.

- ½ teaspoon liquid stevia = 1 cup of sugar.

- Baked goods often depend on sugar to provide structure and moisture. It will take a ton of experimentation to produce a decent baked good that relies only on stevia and no other sweeteners. We look to replace the same volume of sugar with pureed fruit, ground nuts or seeds, finely ground coconut flakes, certified gluten-free rolled oats, and quinoa flakes. All of these will change the result of your baked good. We encourage you to experiment!

- Add extra salt when working with stevia. The salt will help balance the flavor.

- Stevia is an acquired taste. If you need to use stevia for health reasons, try cutting out all other sugar for a few weeks. It will help your palate become accustomed to the flavor and aftertaste.

Recommended Brands:

- **NuNaturals stevia far surpasses the other brands. Their products do not carry a strong bitter aftertaste. We especially love their Liquid Vanilla Stevia.**

- **Sweetleaf is second only to NuNaturals in flavor.**

Xylitol:

Xylitol is a natural sugar alcohol sweetener. It can be used in most recipes that call for refined cane sugar.

Pros: Xylitol has the same sweetness as sugar, but contains fewer calories and is significantly lower on the glycemic index. It is often touted as an alternative sweetener for individuals dealing with candida. It is used in gum because it is less likely to cause tooth decay than sugar.

Cons: Can cause stomach discomfort if eaten in excess.

Baking Tips:

- Xylitol, in most cases, can be exchanged for refined table sugar cup for cup in recipes.

- We noticed one very unique characteristic of xylitol: When we removed our recipes from the oven, they were often too moist. However, twenty-four hours later, that same baked good developed the perfect moisture level. Therefore, we recommend when you use xylitol to plan a day ahead. Once your baked good has cooled, cover and leave it at room temperature for a day.

- Xylitol may change the texture of your baked goods. We noticed it had a tendency to add a gummy texture to a few of our cookie recipes.

- Xylitol has a bit of an artificial flavor if used in excess. Baking usually hides this flavor but if you notice it, simply back off of the amount used.

- Xylitol can be used to make sugar-free powdered sugar. Due to its strong flavor, we suggest combining it with other strong flavors to make frostings.

- Xylitol is not recommended in recipes containing yeast.

Erythritol Crystals:

Erythritol is a sugar alcohol found naturally in fruits and some fermented foods. Like xylitol, it won't cause tooth decay. Our knowledge and experience with this sugar is limited. We do not recommend the use of this sugar in our baked goods as we did not test it in all of the recipes. If you prefer to use it, here's what we know:

Pros: It does not cause blood sugar spikes like sugar does.

Cons: It is generally derived from corn, which many are sensitive to.

Baking Tips:

- In most cases, erythritol can be used cup for cup in baking applications but this amount may need to be to be adjusted as it is less sweet than sugar.

- We noticed that this sugar attributed much less moisture in our baked goods.

- Erythritol is white in color and will not change the color of your baked goods.

Liquid Sugars

Honey:

There is a big difference between raw honey, which you can often find locally, and the processed honey you find at the grocery store. The former is a natural sweetener full of vitamins and minerals. The latter is devoid of nutritional value and may contain high fructose corn syrup.

Pros: Raw honey, as noted, is a nutritional powerhouse and is considered one of nature's superfoods. It is much lower on the glycemic index than sugar or highly processed honey.

Cons: Raw, local honey is often expensive. Honey should not be given to infants.

Baking Tips:

- For every cup of granulated sugar, use ¾ cup of honey. Reduce the liquid ingredients by 2 tablespoons, and you may need to add ¼ teaspoon of baking soda to reduce the acidity of the honey.

- Honey can make some gluten-free baked goods too chewy. We experienced this in a few of our muffin recipes when we tried replacing maple syrup with honey. Replacing sugar with honey in crispy recipes may result in a softer product.

- Honey is extremely sweet, therefore less is usually needed in most recipes.

Recommended Brand:
- **Big Tree Farms has a variety of flavors of honey.**

Brown Rice Syrup:

Brown rice syrup is derived from cooked rice that has been broken down by enzymes. The liquid is strained and cooked down to a thick consistency. Brown rice syrup is thicker than many other liquid sweeteners.

Pros: Brown rice syrup breaks down in the body slower than sugar and will not cause as intense of a blood sugar spike.

Cons: Brown rice syrup is slightly lower than sugar on the glycemic index, thus it is not the best option for diabetics. Some brands contain barley and therefore are not gluten-free. It is important to read the ingredients list carefully.

Baking Tips:

- Its mild flavor works well in most baking applications.

- Can be used as a replacement for honey, agave nectar and maple syrup, although each will impart a slightly unique flavor.

- For every cup of granulated sugar, you can replace with 1¼ cups of brown rice syrup, reducing another liquid in the recipe by ¼ cup.

Recommended Brand:
- **Lundberg Family Farms**

Coconut Nectar:

Coconut nectar is similar to coconut palm sugar. It is lower on the glycemic index than sugar, and is often used in raw food recipes.

Pros: Coconut nectar is low glycemic and nutrient dense.

Cons: It is expensive and not everyone loves the mild flavor. Due to its high cost, we have experimented very little with this sweetener and can only offer a few tips.

Baking Tips:

- Can be used as a replacement for honey in baked goods, but has a milder flavor. For those with a strong sweet tooth, this might not be the best sweetener. However, for those of you who don't need your cookies to be super sweet, this is a great option!

- Use a 1:1 ratio when replacing other liquid sweeteners.

Recommended Brand:
- **Big Tree Farms**

Maple Syrup:

Made from the sap of the maple tree, it has a delicious flavor that we love to use in our baked goods.

Pros: It has a high concentration of minerals and is sweet enough that a little goes a long way.

Cons: Like many other natural sweeteners, it is expensive. It is higher on the glycemic index than coconut nectar and is not a great option for diabetics.

Baking Tips:
- Can be used in a 1:1 ratio with other liquid sweeteners. Just remember it's very sweet and that less may be more.

- In general, you replace a cup of granulated sugar with ¾ cup of maple syrup. You may need to reduce the other liquids in the recipe by a small amount (up to 3 tablespoons).

Molasses:

Molasses is what remains behind after the processing of cane sugar. It can come in three varieties: mild, dark and blackstrap. We recommend using organic blackstrap molasses in your baking. Blackstrap molasses has a higher nutritional value compared with both regular molasses and sugar and contains iron, magnesium, zinc, calcium, copper, phosphorus, and potassium.

Pros: Blackstrap molasses is high in iron and many other vitamins and minerals. No other sweetener imparts quite the same unique flavor.

Cons: Blackstrap molasses should only be used in recipes where you want that strong flavor. It often needs to be combined with another sweetener to neutralize the bitter flavor.

Baking Tips:
- We love using molasses in conjunction with strongly flavored flours, like buckwheat.

- It tastes wonderful in breads, cookies and cakes.

- Often works best when combined with another sweetener.

- Will add a dark rich color to baked goods.

Recommended Brand:
- **Plantation Unsulphured Blackstrap Molasses**

Agave Nectar:

Agave nectar is a hot topic of debate these days. While it was originally recommended for diabetics due to being low on the glycemic index, recent research suggests that it may be no better for you than high fructose corn syrup. Due to this controversy and lack of strong evidence either way, we tend to avoid it in our baking. It can be found in light, dark, amber and raw varieties, each of which will give your baked goods a slightly different flavor.

Pros: Agave nectar is lower on the glycemic index than refined sugar. It is also very sweet so you can often use less in your recipes than you might with other sweeteners.

Cons: The ultimate safety of commercial agave nectar is under debate and we recommend individuals do their own research. The quality of the brand is extremely important and there are many low quality brands on the market. If using it, we recommend you buy an organic brand that you trust.

Baking Tips:

- Most brands of agave work well to make candy, which usually requires a high temperature. We have used it to make caramel, toffee and more.

- Agave is thinner than some of the other liquid sweeteners.

- Agave has a sweet but neutral flavor that works well in most recipes.

- Can be used as a replacement for honey in most baked goods. The neutral flavor will not change the overall integrity of your recipe.

Recommended Brands:
- **Madhava**
- **Wholesome Sweeteners**

Yacon Syrup:

Yacon syrup comes from the South American tuber of the same name. It is similar in flavor to molasses, and is a good low-glycemic option.

Pros: A good option for diabetics and those on an anti-candida diet.

Cons: Once again, like other natural sweeteners, it is expensive and not often found in regular grocery stores.

Baking Tips:
- Use in a 1:1 ratio as a substitute for molasses.

Recommended Brand:
- **Navitas Naturals**

You don't like using xanthan gum in your recipes? Here's how to replace it:

- **Guar Gum:** Use an equal amount of guar gum. The two work almost exactly the same, and we have not noticed a difference in our recipes based on which we used. Guar gum is often preferred by individuals with sensitivities to corn.

- **1 tablespoon ground flax seed meal + 1 tablespoon ground chia seeds (or whole psyllium husks) + 6 tablespoons boiling water (or room temperature full-fat canned coconut milk):** Flax, chia, and psyllium all have incredible binding properties. By mixing 1 tablespoon of ground flax seed meal with 3 tablespoons of hot or boiling water, you'll end up with an "egg" that helps bind your ingredients together and replace an actual egg. This is usually mixed in with the wet ingredients after it has had a few minutes to form a gel. But one flax egg usually isn't enough to bind entire recipes together. You often need to add another egg made with ground chia or whole psyllium husks.

There are a number of methods for using these ingredients to replace xanthan gum. In our recipes, we have specified which ones worked equally well with psyllium husks or chia seeds. If the recipe does not specify that you can use either, it is best to only use the ingredient specified. In some cases, the two cannot be used interchangeably.

> **Recommended Brands:**
> - **Flax Seeds: Navitas Naturals, Shiloh Farms**
> - **Chia Seeds: Navitas Naturals, Shiloh Farms**
> - **Whole Psyllium Husks: Yerba Prima**

The bigger your baked good is the more help it will need to hold it together. Something like a cookie might be able to get away with just one flax egg, half a flax egg or may not even need one.

In recipes like cakes, a full tablespoon each of flax and chia or flax and psyllium is needed. In that case, you'll need a total of 6 tablespoons of boiling water. Bread recipes require even more and in that case we often use up to ¼ cup of psyllium husks in some recipes. You will need to rely on experimentation here, as this is not an exact science. This process will make your recipes moister and fluffier but may not be your desired result.

If you're making a recipe that requires cold ingredients like our Buttermilk Biscuits or Curry Scones, you can use room temperature full-fat canned coconut milk instead of boiling water.

Replacing Common Ingredients

How to replace dairy:

To replace 1 cup butter: Fat has a number of functions in baked goods. It can help add flavor, leaven batters, contribute flakiness and tenderness, and prevent sticking. According to its purpose and considering differing melting points, you'll want to choose the following option that best fits the baked goods you're making:

- **1 cup Earth Balance Buttery Spread (Soy Free option available):** All of our recipes that call for butter have been tested with Earth Balance Soy-Free Buttery Spread. We do not recommend using other types of margarine as our testers reported disastrous results.

- **1 cup shortening (Spectrum Organic Palm Shortening is soy free):** Shortening can generally be used to replace butter, but you'll lose some of that delicious buttery flavor. For recipes in our book that call for shortening, it's best to stick with that as the other options have lower melting points. If a cookie recipe calls for shortening and you use butter, Earth Balance, coconut oil, or oil, it will likely spread too quickly and make a large, flat cookie.

- **1 cup coconut oil:** This is a great substitute for butter. Coconut oil's melting point is slightly lower than butter, but in general, this is a good allergen-free replacement.

Recommended Brand:
- **Garden of Life**
- **1 cup oil:** When melted butter is called for in a recipe, any mild flavored oil, such as canola, grapeseed, extra light olive oil, or melted coconut oil can be used. However, in recipes where you cream the butter, you cannot use an oil. The process of creaming the butter creates air pockets that help create tender, flaky baked goods. Oil will not offer this structure.

- **Applesauce:** To reduce the amount of fat in a recipe, you can sub in applesauce or other pureed fruits. Start with a smaller amount (replace ¼ cup of the fat with ¼ cup of applesauce), and increase as you like. Baked goods made with applesauce will be more moist, less flaky and may require a longer baking time.

To replace 1 cup milk: A quick note for those that can eat dairy products. Keep the following rule in mind when baking with dairy. Fat creates tenderness and moisture. The higher the fat content, usually the better the baked good. The options are:

- **1 cup full-fat canned coconut milk:** Our all time favorite milk to bake with is coconut milk. The high fat content gives a very rich result.

Recommended Brand:
- **We found that Thai Kitchen contains more cream than any other brand. However, Native Forest coconut milk contains only traces of BPA in its** can, while other brands may contain more.

- **1 cup almond, hemp, or soy milk:** These higher-protein milks help add structure to your recipe. This will aid in helping your baked good rise without collapsing.

- **1 cup rice milk, water, or fruit juice:** These substitutes are more like the equivalent of adding fat-free milk, but without the protein. Depending on the flavor profile you're looking for, all of these options are effective. It can be fun to replace milk with juice in white cakes for a new flavor.

To replace 1 cup buttermilk: Buttermilk is a cultured dairy product that adds moisture and tanginess to your baked goods. When buttermilk is heated, the bacteria in it convert a portion of the milk's sugar into acid. Acid is the ingredient for success. Acid will make your baking powder and baking soda *thrive*. To make your own:

- Mix 1 cup of the milk (any variety, dairy or nondairy) + 1 tablespoon of lemon juice, apple cider vinegar, or 1¾ teaspoons of cream of tartar. Stir together and set aside for a few minutes until it begins to curdle.

To replace heavy cream in recipes: Heavy (Full-Fat) Canned Coconut Milk. This works cup for cup in the place of heavy cream in baked goods.

Recommended Brands:
- **Thai Kitchen**
- **Native Forest**

To replace 1 cup cream cheese or sour cream: There are a variety of soy cream cheeses and sour creams on the market. For those who don't use soy or prefer to make your own, here's what we like to do:

- **Cashew cream cheese/sour cream:** To make approximately 1 cup of cream cheese, soak 1½ cups raw cashews in water for at least 4 hours. Rinse and drain, then puree in a food processor along with ¾ teaspoon apple cider vinegar, 1½ teaspoons lemon juice, and ¼ teaspoon salt. Add milk 1 teaspoon at a time until desired consistency is reached.

To replace 1 cup yogurt:

- 1 cup unsweetened applesauce or other fruit puree

- 1 cup non-dairy yogurt

- 1 cup cashew sour cream, thinned to the desired consistency with milk

Avoiding Dairy in Chocolate:

Most brands of chocolate chips are made with dairy. We love Enjoy Life Foods Chocolate Chips and Chocolate Chunks as they are free of gluten, dairy and soy.

How to replace eggs:

Eggs work wonders in gluten-free recipes. We love using them because they work as binders, leaveners, and also help your baked goods dry inside. This can create a light and fluffy cake that won't fall apart. However, there are many of us that can't or choose not to eat eggs. There are many options for replacing eggs:

To mimic the binding properties of egg try any of the following:

Flax, Chia or Psyllium Egg: Replace 1 egg with 1 tablespoon of ground flax seed meal, ground chia seeds, or whole psyllium husks. Stir in 3 tablespoons of boiling water and let sit. For flax and chia seed meal, you can let it sit longer, but psyllium will congeal too much, so you want to stir and then add it to your wet ingredients immediately. This option helps bind ingredients together, which is why we also use this substitution for xanthan gum, as described earlier. Because this will not provide the leavening properties of eggs, you can add a small amount of baking powder if you want a better rise (½ teaspoon).

Tapioca Gel: To keep your recipes from crumbling, you can also use 1 tablespoon tapioca starch mixed with ¼ cup of warm water

Applesauce: 4 tablespoons of unsweetened applesauce, fruit puree, or pureed white or garbanzo beans plus 1 teaspoon baking powder. This will make recipes more moist than an egg will, so adjust your baking time as needed.

Ener-G Egg Replacer: Follow the directions on the box.

To mimic just the leavening properties of egg (make things rise):

- 1 teaspoon baking powder + 1 tablespoon water + 1 tablespoon apple cider vinegar

- To mimic egg whites, which create an incredible rise:

It is not recommended to replace more than 2 egg whites in a recipe. Some recipes, like our Gingerbread Angelfood Cake, are impossible to make without eggs.

Agar agar: Mix 1 tablespoon agar agar powder (not the flakes) into 1 tablespoon of water. Beat, put in the fridge for 15 minutes, then beat again before using in your recipe.

Eggs have a magical ability to deal with high levels of fat in recipes. For example, our Flaky Pie Crust and Nilla-Style Wafers depend on eggs for their texture. Removing the eggs will make both of these recipes extremely gummy. In gluten-free baking we suggest you avoid removing eggs from high fat recipes such as these.

How to replace corn:

We do not use cornstarch in our baking. However, we do use xanthan gum, which is often derived from corn. This can be easily replaced using our suggestions as noted earlier. Believe it or not, baking powder may also contain corn. Hain's featherlight baking powder is corn free. You can also make your own baking powder:

Baking Powder Recipe: to make 1 tablespoon of baking powder, combine:

1 teaspoon baking soda + 2 teaspoons cream of tartar + 1 teaspoon tapioca or arrowroot starch. Use immediately.

Vanilla Extract: Our favorite brand of pure vanilla extract is Simply Organic Pure Vanilla Extract. It is derived from corn, but according to the company, the distillation process makes it corn free. However, some brands can contain corn and making your own is easy!

Combine 6 vanilla beans and 2 cups of vodka into a sealed container. Store in a dark space for 2 months, shaking every so often. After the 2 months, use vanilla extract in all your recipes! Vanilla beans can be re-used to make a second and third batch.

Powdered Sugar: Many commercial brands of powdered sugar can contain corn. Trader Joe's is an exception. You can make your own powdered sugar using our recipe in the frosting section.

Earth Balance products can contain corn. Read our dairy substitution section for alternatives to butter and Earth Balance.

Ask the Expert

Kim Maes is an expert in allergen-free baking. In addition to writing the popular blog, CookItAllergyFree.com, she developed a must-have iPhone and iPad app for those with food allergies and intolerances. Using her app, you can look up any ingredient and find a suitable substitution. Kim's knowledge in this area is astounding.

How long have you been baking gluten-free? I began baking gluten-free more than six years ago when my oldest son was diagnosed with celiac disease. When my husband was diagnosed shortly thereafter, we converted our entire home to be gluten-free.

Do you remember the first thing you ever baked gluten-free? How did it turn out? The very first thing I attempted to make gluten-free were banana muffins. I was not initially wowed with the results. I began to realize that there is a true science to gluten-free baking. The chemistry and biology major in me took hold and I began experimenting. I figured out that once you learn the basics of ratios, types of higher protein flours versus starches, and the balance of wet to dry ingredients, there is no stopping the amazing results you can have.

Do you ever use commercial gluten-free all-purposes mixes? I prefer to make my own blends, depending on what recipe I am making. However, there are times that I will just use a quick mix. I usually achieve the best results with either Pamela's All-Purpose Baking Mix, King Arthur's Gluten-Free Multi-Purpose Flour, or the Pure Pantry Organic Baking Mix.

What are the top three things every new baker should know?

1. Always have *all* of your ingredients at room temperature; this will make all of the difference in your results and how your ingredients react with each other.

2. Make sure that your baking soda and baking powder have not expired. It is difficult enough to get gluten-free baked goods to get a good rise, so this step is crucial to your baking. To test if baking powder is still good: combine 1 teaspoon of baking powder with ⅓ cup hot water. If it bubbles, it is still good. If not, replace it. To test if baking soda is still good: add ½ teaspoon of baking soda to 4 Tablespoons of white vinegar. This should fizz up. If not, discard it.

3. Verify your oven temperature with an oven thermometer. A 10 degree temperature difference in either direction can make a big difference. If you know, for instance, that your oven runs 10 degrees hotter than you can adjust for that.

Do you have any money saving tips for gluten-free bakers? Buy your flours in bulk sizes. If you are going to be going through a lot of flour, you will find such a dramatic difference in price between buying 5 individual 1 pound bags of flour versus buying 1 single 5 pound bag of it. Check prices online and look for sales in stores and online. Also, if you sign up for your favorite companies' newsletters or like their Facebook Pages, you often get coupons and discounts. I never thought I would be able to go through big bags of flour. But I was surprised at how quickly I can use them up now.

What tips would you give for someone wanting to convert a family favorite recipe to gluten-free? Substituting ingredients is also about trial-and-error. A replacement that may work in one recipe may not work well in another. Take notes. The best way to convert recipes is to view it as an adventure. The times that the recipe does not turn out quite right just may give you a brand new idea for a completely different recipe. I look at each mistake as a lesson.

What type of recipes do you typically use buckwheat in? If a recipe calls for buckwheat, are there any other flours that you would sub in with similar results? I use buckwheat flour in crepes, pancakes, even granola bars. I make buckwheat date muffins that turn out nicely. Teff flour seems to sub out nicely with buckwheat. The protein structure and weight of teff and buckwheat

flours are similar enough that they seem to work fairly nicely in place of each other.

What are your top three favorite flours to work with and why? My favorite flours to work with are almond flour, millet flour and superfine brown rice flour. They all add a nice bit of protein and fiber to recipes and help avoid the blood sugar spike that can happen with baked goods when using more of the starchy blends.

What are your top three favorite types of recipes to bake and why? The recipes I bake most often are ones that help me to get quick and protein-filled breakfasts into my family on busy mornings. On many mornings I will make a grain-free puffed pancake made with almond flour. I also make an oatmeal cinnamon breakfast cake with certified gluten-free oats that I throw together the night before, up until the point of baking, and then I throw it in the oven in the morning while everyone is getting dressed. I make variety of muffins as well that are either grain-free or use high-protein flour blends.

What kind of gluten-free recipes would you suggest for a beginner to start with? A basic muffin or quickbread recipe is a great way to practice with different flours. You then can experiment with different add-ins and alternative flours.

Do you bake by weight or volume? When subbing one flour for another, do you do it by weight or volume? I tend to do both equally. I keep my kitchen scale out and I do use it on a regular basis when subbing one flour out for another. However, on recipes that I am very familiar with, I tend to go by volume. I know that weight is technically much more accurate, but I do not find a drastic enough difference in many of my recipes by doing it by weight.

What do you generally use as egg replacers in baking? If you use more than one, how do you decide which to use in a recipe? For cakes, muffins and quickbread-type recipes, I use the following replacement per egg:

Mix together in small bowl: 1½ Tbsp unsweetened applesauce with ¾ tsp additional baking powder with 1 Tbsp warm water and with ¾ tsp Ener-G Egg Replacer. Use this mixture where you would add eggs.

For cookies I use the following per egg:
2 tablespoons water + 1 tablespoon oil + ½ teaspoon baking powder, beaten together until smooth

What kind of dairy free replacements do you like to bake with? Do you think the changes affect the texture and flavor? For dairy-free baking, my favorite replacement is coconut milk. I have found that the canned full-fat coconut milk adds a much richer flavor and texture. And the refrigerated coconut milk found in the carton adds a milder flavor and texture. I actually use both the canned and cartoned versions, depending on what I have on hand or what I am trying to replace in a recipe. When I am replacing something like half-and-half or heavy cream I go with the canned version and sometimes I will even only use just the creamed portion on top if my goal is a really decadent result.

What differences have you noticed between tapioca starch, potato starch and arrowroot starch? How do you decide which you want to use in a recipe? I have found, for the most part, that you can use the three different starches fairly interchangeably.

Chapter 2

Sorghum Flour

a.k.a. Sweet White Sorghum or Jowar Flour

Sorghum flour is the unsung hero of gluten-free baking. While it doesn't get as much attention as the other flours, it's one of our favorites. The taste most resembles wheat flour, with a mild flavor and very slight sour aftertaste. It provides the much-needed structure to recipes and works great as a background flour. Basically, while other flours might provide a unique texture and/or strong flavor, sorghum quietly does its job.

Brand Comparison:

We did not notice much difference between the various brands of sorghum flours. We've tested our recipes out successfully with Nuts.com, Dakota Prairie and Bob's Red Mill.

Best Flours to Substitute for Sorghum Flour:

Millet, Garbanzo, Quinoa, Teff, Brown Rice, and White Rice Flour: Because sorghum flour works best as a background flour, it's easy to substitute in and out of recipes. These flour replacements will rise well. Just remember that the unique attributes of these flours (textures, flavors, colors, etc.) will be noticeable. We have found that brown rice flour works best as a substitute as it carries a similar weight to sorghum.

Buckwheat Flour: Buckwheat can be used instead of sorghum, but the result will be dense and have the strong, earthy flavor of buckwheat. You may need to adjust your liquid as buckwheat has the tendency to absorb more liquid.

Sorghum Flour Tips

- For simplicity's sake, we've tried to use as few flours as possible for each recipe in this chapter (in many cases, just the sorghum flour and a starch). However, you can achieve better texture and flavor through a mix of three different flour varieties. For instance, in our Pineapple Upside Down Cake, we use a blend of sorghum flour, brown rice flour, and potato starch. We originally tried it with just sorghum flour and potato starch, but found the resulting cake to be heavy. Adding the third flour created a lighter texture.

- Most of our sorghum flour recipes can be replaced with all-purpose mixes. But rather than just replacing the sorghum flour, replace all of the flours and starches with the all-purpose mix. For instance, if the recipe calls for 1 cup of sorghum flour, 1 cup of brown rice flour, and 1 cup of potato starch, replace that with 3 cups of all-purpose mix.

- Sorghum flour works wonderfully in breads, muffins, and other whole-grain-type recipes. When combined with other lighter flours and starches (e.g. white rice, tapioca, arrowroot or potato starch), sorghum can create a lighter, fluffier texture. The higher the percentage of starch in any recipe the lighter the result of the baked good.

- On a heavy to light flour scale, sorghum is right smack in the middle.

Fun Uses for Sorghum:

- It makes amazing gravy! Use sorghum flour and tapioca or arrowroot starch in a 1:1 ratio to thicken your favorite gravy recipes, just as you would with wheat flour. Sorghum can be used exclusively to make gravy, but we've found we prefer the flavor and texture of the gravy when sorghum is mixed with a starch.

Cheesy Cornbread Balls

. . . .

Serve these snacks hot with marinara sauce and they'll disappear quickly. Leftovers can be frozen and repurposed to make cornbread stuffing. For the cheddar cheese, we enjoy Daiya, but play around with whatever type of cheese you like best.

Yield: 16 cornbread balls

DIRECTIONS:

1. Lightly oil a cookie sheet. Preheat the oven to 425 degrees F.

2. In a small bowl, stir apple cider vinegar into milk and set aside to let curdle.

3. In a large bowl, whisk together the cornmeal, sorghum flour, potato starch, flax seed meal, chia seeds, baking powder, baking soda, and salt. Set aside.

4. Whisk the maple syrup and applesauce into the curdled milk, and then pour that into the dry ingredients, stirring until completely mixed. Stir in the cheese.

5. Form balls in the palm of your hand (about 2-3 tablespoons each), and bake for 15-18 minutes, until balls begin to brown lightly.

These are best when eaten warm from the oven.

INGREDIENTS:

½ cup milk

1½ teaspoons apple cider vinegar

175 grams cornmeal (1 ¼ cups)

65 grams sorghum flour (½ lightly filled cup)

43 grams potato starch (¼ cup)

1 tablespoon ground flax seed meal

1 tablespoon ground chia seeds or whole psyllium husks

1 teaspoon baking powder

½ teaspoon baking soda

¾ teaspoon salt

2 tablespoons honey

¼ cup unsweetened applesauce

1 cup grated cheddar cheese

Apple Cinnamon Waffles

These are some of our favorite waffles. We top them with thinly sliced apples before cooking and this yields a sweet breakfast treat.

Yield: 4-5 waffles

Directions:

1. In a large bowl, whisk together the sorghum flour, potato starch, sugar, baking powder, salt, and cinnamon.

2. In a medium-sized bowl, whisk together the applesauce, oil, vanilla, and coconut milk. Pour the wet ingredients into the dry and stir completely.

3. Spray waffle iron with oil to keep from sticking. Pour batter onto middle of waffle iron and spread out to the edges with a spoon. The batter will be thick. Quickly place apple slices on the batter and close the iron.

4. Cook on the highest setting so that the waffle gets crispy on the outside.

These can be frozen for later use.

Ingredients:

162 grams sorghum flour (1¼ lightly filled cups)

86 grams potato starch (½ cup)

2 tablespoons unrefined granulated sugar

2 teaspoons baking powder

½ teaspoon salt

1½ teaspoons cinnamon

¼ cup unsweetened applesauce

2 tablespoons mild flavored oil

1 teaspoon pure vanilla extract

1½ cups full-fat canned coconut milk

1 medium apple, peeled, cored, and sliced very thinly

Spinach & Shallot Soufflés

Despite their fancy appearance, these are quick to throw together. Serve for breakfast, lunch or dinner.

Yield: Six ramekins

Directions:

1. Preheat oven to 375 degrees F. Butter or oil six ramekins. Place ramekins on a baking sheet and set aside.

2. In a saucepan, whisk together the butter, sorghum flour, milk, vinegar, nutritional yeast, salt, garlic powder, and pepper. Cook over low heat and allow the mixture to thicken slightly. Remove from heat.

3. Whisk in the 3 large eggs. Stir in the spinach and shallots (if using fresh spinach, stir until it wilts).

4. Beat 4 egg whites in a clean bowl until they form stiff peaks.

5. Using a spatula, gently fold the soufflé batter into the prepared egg whites a little at a time. Be careful to not completely deflate the egg whites.

6. Pour the batter into the six buttered ramekins. Place baking sheet in oven quickly and bake 30 minutes. Do not open the oven during this time as it may cause the soufflés to deflate.

7. Serve hot. Soufflés will begin to fall as they cool.

Ingredients:

⅛ cup butter or oil

32 grams sorghum flour (3 tablespoons)

½ cup + 2 tablespoons milk

1 teaspoon vinegar

3½ tablespoons nutritional yeast

1 teaspoon salt

1 tablespoon garlic powder

¼ teaspoon pepper

3 large eggs

½ cup baby spinach

1-2 small shallots, finely minced

4 large egg whites, beaten to stiff peaks

Spicy Chipotle Jalapeño & Corn Muffins

Chipotle powder gives these muffins a smoky and spicy flavor that's offset by the sweetness of maple syrup. Combine them with scrambled tofu and spinach for a hearty breakfast or enjoy them alone as an afternoon snack. You can adjust the amount of chipotle powder to your personal preference.

Yield: One dozen muffins

Directions:

1. Preheat the oven to 375 degrees F.

2. In a large bowl, whisk together the sorghum flour, tapioca starch, cornmeal, chipotle powder, baking powder, baking soda, and salt. Set aside.

3. In a medium-sized bowl, mix the flax seed meal, ground chia, oil, applesauce, milk, and maple syrup. Add wet ingredients to dry and stir until completely mixed. Stir in the corn and jalapeño.

5. Grease muffin tins and fill to the top with batter. Bake for 22 minutes.

6. While muffins are baking, whisk together 2 tablespoons of maple syrup and ½ teaspoon of milk. When the muffins are done, take them out and brush the tops generously with the maple syrup wash.

7. Put back in the oven for another 1-2 minutes. Let cool for a few minutes before removing muffins to a cooling rack. Serve warm.

Store in an airtight container in the fridge or freeze for later use.

Ingredients:

130 grams sorghum flour (1 lightly filled cup)

90 grams tapioca starch (¾ cup)

41 grams cornmeal (¼ cup)

1½ teaspoons chipotle powder or to taste

1 teaspoon baking powder

1 teaspoon baking soda

1 teaspoon salt

1 tablespoon ground flax seed meal

1 tablespoon ground chia seeds

¼ cup mild flavored oil

½ cup unsweetened applesauce

1 cup plus 2 tablespoons milk

2 tablespoons maple syrup

1 cup corn (frozen and thawed or canned, drained)

2 tablespoons minced jalapeño

Maple Syrup Wash:

2 tablespoons maple syrup

½ teaspoon milk

PB & J Snack Crackers

These tea biscuits can easily be frozen and put in your lunchbox (or your child's) for lunch. They will defrost within a few hours.

Yield: One dozen crackers

Directions:

1. Preheat oven to 350 degrees F. Set aside one lightly greased cookie sheet.

2. Pour boiling water over flax seed meal and let sit while you whisk together the dry ingredients.

3. Whisk together sorghum flour, brown rice flour, tapioca starch, salt, baking soda, and baking powder. Set aside.

4. Add honey and oil to flax mix. Stir into dry ingredients until completely mixed. Stir in the extra 32 grams of sorghum flour and knead into a ball.

5. Roll dough out to ⅛" thickness between two pieces of parchment paper. Cut the dough into circles with a biscuit cutter (or bottom of a glass if you don't have a biscuit cutter). Roll up remaining dough into a ball and repeat until all the dough is gone.

6. Place half of the circles on the cookie sheet. Spread a thin layer of peanut butter and jelly in the middle of the circles, then top with another circle and pinch the edges closed.

7. Bake for 16 minutes. Remove to a cooling rack and allow to cool completely.

Store in an airtight container in the freezer.

Ingredients:

2 tablespoons ground flax seed meal

½ cup boiling water

130 grams sorghum flour (1 lightly filled cup)

32 grams brown rice flour (¼ lightly filled cup)

60 grams tapioca starch (½ cup)

1 teaspoon salt

½ teaspoon baking soda

1 teaspoon double acting baking powder

2 tablespoons honey

5 Tablespoons mild flavored oil

32 grams sorghum flour (¼ lightly filled cup)

Peanut butter (room temperature)

Jelly

Butternut Squash Pot Pie with Vegan Crust

· ·

This vegan crust was an easy collaboration. Our testers agree that the filling goes perfectly with the crust.

Yield: Six servings

DIRECTIONS:

1. Heat olive oil in a large soup pot on medium heat. Add onion and cook for 5 minutes. While the onions are cooking, whisk together the tapioca starch and broth. Turn heat up to high and add the broth to the onions along with the carrots, potato, and butternut squash.

2. Once the broth begins to boil, turn the heat down to a gentle simmer. Add garbanzo beans, peas, cumin, cinnamon, garlic powder, and pepper. Cover with a lid and simmer for 15 minutes.

3. Spoon the filling into a large pie pan or 8 x 8 inch baking dish. Now it's time to make your pie crust.

4. Preheat the oven to 425 degrees F.

5. In a small bowl, stir together the flax seed meal, psyllium husks, and coconut milk. Set aside for a few minutes.

6. In a large mixing bowl, whisk together the sorghum flour, tapioca starch, sugar, baking powder, salt, and cinnamon. Cut in the shortening. Stir in the coconut milk and flax mixture until a dough is formed. Alternatively, you can make this in a food processor, blending the shortening in

with the dry ingredients, then adding the coconut milk and flax mix.

7. Roll the dough out between two pieces of parchment paper. Once the dough is the size of your baking dish, the best way to transfer it to the dish is by rolling it up like sushi, and then unrolling it over the dish.

8. Bake for 25 minutes. Serve hot.

Store in an airtight container in the fridge or freeze for later use.

INGREDIENTS:

BUTTERNUT SQUASH FILLING:

1 tablespoon olive oil

1 medium yellow onion, diced

2 tablespoons tapioca starch

1 ½ cups vegetable broth

3 medium carrots, diced

1 medium potato, diced

½ small butternut squash, seeded, peeled, and diced

1 15-ounce can garbanzo beans, rinsed and drained

½ cup peas

1 teaspoon ground cumin

1 teaspoon ground cinnamon

1 teaspoon garlic powder

1 teaspoon freshly ground black pepper

VEGAN POT PIE CRUST:

1 tablespoon ground flax seed meal

1 tablespoon whole psyllium husks

½ cup full-fat canned coconut milk (room temperature)

65 grams sorghum flour (½ lightly filled cup)

90 grams tapioca starch (¾ cup)

1 tablespoon unrefined granulated sugar

1 teaspoon baking powder

½ teaspoon salt

½ teaspoon cinnamon

½ cup shortening

Yeast-Free, Vegan Sandwich Bread

While writing this cookbook, we were determined to have good sandwich bread recipes for everyone. This is for those of you who can't have eggs or yeast. With a crispy crust and chewy interior, we think you'll enjoy a slice of toast again. We ignored the rules and used teff flour instead of rice flour, and we love the texture it gives to this bread. I give thanks to Christine Holzmann for her help getting the recipe perfect. After I came up with my initial recipe, Christine went through a number of tests in her own kitchen to find the right combination of ingredients. This recipe is as much hers as it is mine.

— Iris

Yield: One 9 x 5 inch loaf

Directions:

1. Preheat the oven to 375 degrees F. Oil a 9 x 5 inch bread pan.

2. In a medium-sized bowl, whisk together the sorghum flour, potato starch, teff flour, sugar, baking powder, baking soda, and salt.

3. In a large bowl, beat together the psyllium husks, applesauce, oil, apple cider vinegar, and water on low speed for 1 minute. Slowly pour in the dry ingredients, increasing the speed to medium and beat for 2 minutes.

4. Scoop the batter into the pan, brush with oil, and smooth out with your fingertips or a spatula. Bake for 70 minutes or until a knife inserted in the middle comes out clean.

5. Remove from oven, turn onto a cooling rack, and let cool for at least an hour before slicing.

Store in an airtight container in the fridge or slice and store in the freezer.

Ingredients:

163 grams sorghum flour (1¼ lightly filled cups)

215 grams potato starch (1¼ cups)

77 grams teff flour (½ lightly filled cup)

¼ cup unrefined granulated sugar

1 teaspoon baking powder

½ teaspoon baking soda

½ teaspoon salt

6 tablespoons whole psyllium husks (ground chia seeds will not work)

⅛ cup unsweetened applesauce

⅛ cup mild flavored oil

½ teaspoon apple cider vinegar

2¼ cups water

Pineapple Upside Down Cake

This gluten-free rendition of a traditional pineapple upside down cake uses the sweetness of pineapple juice as a natural sweetener. A couple of tablespoons of maple syrup and raisins enhance the flavor without being overly sweet.

Yield: One 8 x 8 inch square cake

DIRECTIONS:

1. Preheat oven to 350 degrees F. Grease an 8 x 8 inch pan. Arrange pineapple rings in the bottom of the pan, cutting in half if necessary to fit as many as you can. Place ¼ cup of raisins in and around the pineapple rings to make a pretty pattern.

2. Gently heat 2 tablespoons of coconut oil and 2 tablespoons of maple syrup on the stove until the coconut oil is just melted. Pour evenly over the pineapples. Set aside.

3. In a large bowl, whisk together sorghum flour, brown rice flour, potato starch, baking powder, baking soda, xanthan gum, cinnamon, nutmeg, and salt.

4. In a small bowl, pour boiling water over flax seed meal. Stir briefly and let sit for a minute. Stir applesauce, 2 tablespoons of maple syrup, ¾ cup of pineapple juice, and vanilla extract into the flax seed mixture.

5. Gently heat remaining 3 tablespoons of coconut oil on the stove until just melted. Stir into the flax seed mixture.

6. Stir flax seed mixture into dry ingredients until completely mixed. Fold in ½ cup of raisins. Pour batter into pan over pineapple rings.

7. Bake for 40 minutes or until a toothpick stuck in the middle comes out clean. Let sit for a couple of minutes before carefully turning over onto a flat surface to cool. Let the cake pan rest upside down briefly before taking it off so all the syrup drips down into the cake.

Serve warm or at room temperature. Store in an airtight container in the fridge or freeze for later use.

INGREDIENTS:

1 20-ounce can pineapple rings in its own juice

¼ cup raisins

2 tablespoons coconut oil

2 tablespoons maple syrup

110 grams sorghum flour (¾ packed cup)

70 grams brown rice flour (½ packed cup)

129 grams potato starch (½ cup + 1 tablespoon)

1 teaspoon baking powder

1 teaspoon baking soda

1 teaspoon xanthan gum

½ teaspoon ground cinnamon

¼ teaspoon ground nutmeg

½ teaspoon salt

2 tablespoons flax seed meal

6 tablespoons boiling water

1 cup unsweetened applesauce

2 tablespoons maple syrup

¾ cup pineapple juice

1 teaspoon pure vanilla extract

3 tablespoons coconut oil

½ cup raisins

1 cup of walnuts

2 tablespoons coconut oil

¼ cup granulated sugar

1 teaspoon cinnamon

Cake:

195 grams sorghum flour (1½ lightly filled cups)

258 grams potato starch (1½ cups)

1 cup unrefined granulated sugar

1 teaspoon xanthan gum

½ teaspoon baking soda

1 tablespoon double acting baking powder

½ teaspoon salt

⅔ cup unsweetened applesauce

⅔ cup mild flavored oil

6 tablespoons milk

1 tablespoon pure vanilla extract

zest of one small lemon

1 tablespoon lemon juice

Lemon Crumb Cake

We love serving this cake for brunch. With just a hint of lemon flavor, it's a nice variation on the typical coffee cake. It's perfectly moist on day one, but has a tendency to dry out after that. This makes it a delicious addition to your breakfast. Instead of granola, crumble a slice of lemon crumb cake into your yogurt.

Yield: One 8 x 8 inch cake

DIRECTIONS:

1. Preheat oven to 350 degrees F. Lightly grease an 8 x 8 inch baking dish.

2. Process topping ingredients in a food processor for about 30 seconds. Set aside.

3. In a large bowl, whisk together sorghum flour, potato starch, sugar, xanthan gum, baking soda, baking powder, and salt.

4. In a medium-sized large bowl, whisk together applesauce, oil, milk, vanilla, lemon zest, and juice.

4. Stir wet ingredients into dry until completely mixed. Pour batter into pan.

5. Pat topping down over batter. Bake for 30 - 35 minutes, until a toothpick inserted in the middle comes out clean. Let cool before serving.

Store in an airtight container in the fridge or freeze for later use.

Ask the Expert

. . . .

Sara Boswell is an expert on the milling and baking properties of sorghum. She has studied under well-known Texas A&M food researcher Lloyd Rooney in the Cereal Grains Quality Lab for the past four years. An opportunity to learn from Sarah is a lucky one. With a BS in Human Nutrition and a MS in Food Science and Technology from Texas A&M University, Sara's knowledge in food science is vast.

How long have you been baking gluten-free? I started baking gluten-free products when I was a sophomore in college. I had been on a gluten-free diet for nearly four years, but had never taken on the challenge of baking for myself. The opportunity came when, as part of a nutrition course, I was tasked with converting a traditional recipe to something that would be safe for a patient on a diet.

Do you ever use commercial gluten-free all-purpose mixes? I use King Arthur's Chocolate Cake Mix for most of my chocolate cakes. It's really nice to save some time using a premix and it's less stressful, especially if baking does not come naturally to you.

What flours do you like to use to make cake? When I do use my own blend to make cakes, I typically use a blend of finely ground white sorghum flour, tapioca flour or potato starch. For each type of cake you can tweak the blend you use depending on how soft of a crumb you are looking for.

Have you noticed a difference in results between white and brown rice flour in baked goods? White and brown rice flour have very different baking properties. Brown rice flour contains the endosperm or hull of the grain; this can cause a darker crumb color and change the aroma of your baked good. Depending on the particle size of the flour, brown rice flour can be grittier than traditional white rice flour.

What flours besides rice do you find work well exchanged for each other? Brown rice flour can usually be replaced with sorghum or millet flour, depending on the recipe. In some recipes you can also exchange potato and tapioca starch. However, this will cause a change in texture.

What are the top three things every new baker should know?

1. Practice makes perfect. Very rarely will you perfect a recipe on your first try. Try not to discouraged if something does not work. You can always make changes to it next time.

2. Quality of your ingredients counts: The particle size and grittiness of the flour you are using can make or break a recipe. It's important to follow suggestions on brands from recipe writers because the same type of product produced by a different company could have a larger or smaller particle size than what is

needed for that recipe. Smaller particle sizes of flour will absorb more moisture, and larger sized particles will absorb less, this is due to the reduced amount of surface area available for water absorption. Volume measurements can also change depending on the particle size. One cup of finely ground flour will differ in weight from one cup of coarsely ground flour.

3. Stay organized: Set out all of the ingredients and equipment that you need in the order that you will need them. If you go into your first baking experiences prepared, it can be much less stressful and help you stay on track.

Do you have any money saving tips for gluten-free bakers? Avoid the really expensive flours or gluten-free mixes. Scout out stores in your area and compare the cost of flours to the bulk online prices. Ask your local grocery store if they offer discounts for purchasing an entire case of a product; sometimes this yields up to 10 percent off. Watch for coupons and sales of your favorite brands and then stock up.

What tips would you give for someone wanting to convert a family favorite recipe to gluten-free? Try to find a similar recipe that is gluten-free and then make adjustments from there. Starting from scratch can be quite frustrating because often times gluten-free recipes will need different water and fat ratios that could be difficult to figure out on your own.

What are your top three favorite flours to work with and why? It would have to be tapioca starch, white sorghum flour and finely ground sumac sorghum bran. Using tapioca and sorghum together creates a nice soft crumb with a neutral flavor that works with sweet or savory recipes. Sumac sorghum bran is more difficult to find, but it can serve as a natural colorant, dietary fiber additive, source of antioxidants, and has a pleasant flavor that is incredibly different from other grains. I love adding this bran to muffins, breads and pancakes.

Can you tell us a bit about sorghum flour? There are many different types and varieties of sorghum. The white, yellow, red, brown, and black varieties all have slightly different flavors and colors. The ideal flour to use in baking is white sorghum. White sorghum will produce a nice light tan crumb color that can be used in both sweet and savory baked items. It's considered a neutral flavor, however, it is distinct from the flavor of the other gluten-free grains. It's a long-running joke at my workplace that I will find a way to use sorghum in just about any recipe imaginable. The only product that I have trouble using sorghum in is yellow pasta, since it gives a slightly tan color to any product you use in it in.

What are your favorite types of recipes to bake and why? My favorite things to make are traditional family recipes like my grandmother's cheese straws. The recipe has been in the family for more than 50 years. Also, cakes with unique flavor combinations provide new challenges for me. At Christmas this year I made a 7-layer chocolate cake with a mascarpone cheese filling and a ganache coating. I'll be honest: it did take me a few hours to make and was a bit of a challenge, but in the end it was worth it. It was the only dessert that had been completely eaten and received glowing reviews from my gluten-eating relatives. My only regret was not getting a good photo. At work, my favorite things to make are breads. I typically make 7 to 10 loaves a day when I am baking. This type of replication baking is calming to me and I enjoy the time I have to think and be creative. I have found that some of my best ideas come to me when I am half-awake at work at 5 a.m. in the morning.

What kind of gluten-free recipes would you suggest for a beginner to start with? Cupcakes are a new baker's best friends. They are very forgiving in terms of technique and flavor (the sweetness helps to cover up any mistakes), do not require large amounts of expensive ingredients, and have a small surface area, which makes it easier to get them to rise and set in place without collapsing.

What's the most challenging recipe you ever developed and why? Bread. Wheat-based breads require large amounts of strong protein to create, which is very difficult to mimic in gluten-free baking. Mimicking the ability of a dough to stretch, trap air molecules during baking, and then to not collapse after the crumb of the bread has baked is a challenge, even for the most skilled bakers.

When looking at gluten-free breads, I want to find a bread with even air cell distribution in the crumb and with air cells that are not too large. Large air bubbles or tunneling in a bread is a sign that the yeast in your bread was not mixed as well as it should have been. I also do not want a bread that collapses and loses volume after baking. A general rule of thumb to those of us in the food industry is "sell more air." This means that you want as much air as possible to give you as large of a loaf as possible to give your consumer a usable bread. One trend that drives me crazy as a gluten-free bread consumer is the small size of the bread loaves sold. I want bread that is large enough for a decent sandwich. If you can master the art of bread baking at home, this can save you quite a bit of money and provide you with a tastier option than what is available at your local store.

Do you bake by weight or volume? I bake strictly by weight. Since it is required for me to do so at work, I do the scaling calculations in my head. When substituting ingredients I typically substitute by weight unless I am substituting a whole grain for a starch (or vice versa).

What kind of dairy-free replacements do you like to bake with? In baking, dairy is typically used for browning or for layering of fat in pastry recipes. Dairy can easily be replaced in most recipes by adding a coating of egg wash towards the end of baking (to create a nice golden crust) or with solid non-dairy fats with oils. It will cause a change in flavor in recipes that call for large amounts of butter, but if you do not tell those who are eating it that it is dairy-free they often will not notice!

What differences have you noticed between tapioca starch, potato starch and arrowroot starch? All three of these starches have different gelatinization (melting temperatures) and water absorption levels. I tend to not use arrowroot because it is very expensive at my local store. Potato is notoriously chewy, more so than tapioca starch. You can typically interchange all three fairly easily with only minor changes to the texture.

Can you give our readers some gluten-free bread making tips? Are there certain flours or other ingredients that you always use when making bread? I am a huge fan of using sorghum flour with xanthan gum in bread. One of the key aspects of making bread is the proofing process when the batter is allowed to rise. You need to have a humid and warm space for the yeast to produce gases and the batter to rise. Unlike traditional bread baking, gluten-free bread should only be allowed to rise once due to the lack of elasticity of the batter.

Can you give our readers some tips in how to get started with making bread without eggs? Use a smaller sized pan called a "pup" loaf. You can find these pans online when you search for "pup loaf pan" and it will produce a small size loaf of bread. This would be very useful for egg free baking because

you would not have as much surface area that the bread would be required to rise in.

Is there anything else you think our readers should know about gluten-free baking? There is always something fun and new to learn when it comes to baking. I love talking about baking methodology with other gluten-free bakers. The more information and results that we share with others the more progress we make in terms of fully understanding gluten- and allergen-free baking.

Chapter 3

Buckwheat Flour

Buckwheat is a gluten-free flour that many people have used prior to going gluten-free. It is often used in combination with wheat to make pancakes and crepes. Buckwheat has an earthy, bold flavor with a hint of molasses and a slightly bitter aftertaste. The flour comes in two varieties: light and dark. The dark variety is more robust and may affect the rise of certain recipes. Thus, we prefer to use the light variety for baking; it has a milder flavor and better rise. We love using it in recipes with equally strong flavors. Regardless of the variety you choose, our Chocolate Coated Brownie Bites and Buckwheat Molasses Bread stand up to buckwheat's robust flavor.

Note: Recipes with mild flavors may be overpowered when buckwheat is added. For example, using buckwheat to make chocolate chip cookies would be a bad idea. In the case of our German Chocolate Cookie Sandwiches, the chocolate flavor is complemented beautifully.

If you prefer to grind your own flour at home, you can buy raw buckwheat groats, which are the seeds of the buckwheat plant. Freshly ground groats will give you a milder flavor. Store bought pre-ground buckwheat flour is roasted to enhance the naturally robust flavor.

Nutritional Highlights:

Despite its name, buckwheat has no relation to wheat. The seeds come from a flowering plant, and are rich in essential amino acids, fatty acids and certain B vitamins. Buckwheat is thought to aid in the regulation of blood glucose, and may help stimulate good bacteria in our guts while decreasing bad bacteria.

Brand Comparison:

There are numerous brands of buckwheat flour available in stores. Our favorite is Dakota Prairie's Light Buckwheat Flour. Bob's Red Mill Buckwheat Flour will work as the next best option in our recipes.

Best flours to substitute for buckwheat flour:

1. Teff: Teff and buckwheat have a similar flavor. Teff is sweeter and also much lighter than buckwheat. It will create a fluffier result. Substitute teff for buckwheat in a 1:1 ratio. You may need to reduce the amount of liquid needed when using teff.

2. Millet, Quinoa, Sorghum, Garbanzo, Brown Rice, and White Rice Flour: All of these flours can be used in a 1:1 ratio with buckwheat. Like teff, they will create a lighter product and you may need to reduce the liquid by a small amount.

3. Amaranth Flour: Although we don't generally recommend amaranth as a substitute because of its strong flavor, you can sub small amounts of amaranth for buckwheat. They are both dense flours and soak up approximately the same amount of liquid. You shouldn't have to adjust the liquid ratio much, if at all.

Buckwheat Flour Tips:

- Buckwheat is a dense flour. It is great for recipes that don't require much rise, such as cookies, bars and brownies. To create light and fluffy cakes, you will need a high percentage of either eggs or starch to counter the heaviness of the flour.

- Spices like nutmeg, cinnamon, cloves and chocolate work well in buckwheat recipes.

- In cookie applications, we found the buckwheat created a chewy texture.

- Buckwheat on its own does not provide a soft texture to baked goods.

Fun uses for buckwheat flour

- Raw buckwheat groats can be made into a porridge very similar to oatmeal.
- Raw buckwheat groats can be soaked, pureed with a little applesauce, oil, and milk, and baked for a flatbread.

Buckwheat Crepes

· ·

We simplified this recipe to its bare bones. No eggs needed! These delicious little crepes are soft with just a touch of crunchiness on the edges. Not too sweet, these can be used in both sweet and savory dishes.

Yield: 8-10 crepes

DIRECTIONS:

1. Whisk ingredients together in a bowl to make a thin batter.

2. Heat and lightly oil a nonstick skillet.

3. Pour ¼ cup of batter into the pan. Lift and tilt the pan so that the batter spreads into a very thin circular shape. Cook roughly one minute and then gently flip and cook the second side.

   Serve stuffed with your favorite filling.

   Note: The range of milk is there because the different brands of flour may soak up a little more or less liquid. Play around with this amount to find what works best for you. If you feel your crepes are a little thick, add more milk.

INGREDIENTS:

101 grams buckwheat flour (¾ lightly filled cup)

43 grams tapioca or arrowroot flour (⅓ cup)

¼ cup liquid sweetener (agave, brown rice syrup, honey, coconut nectar)

½ teaspoon salt

1¼ - 1½ cups milk or water

Buckwheat Tortillas

Tortillas are a cinch to make, even gluten-free ones. These tortillas will flex and bend, making a good wrap. This version uses buckwheat, an earthy flavor that pairs well with most savory fillings.

Yield: One dozen tortillas

DIRECTIONS:

1. In a large bowl, combine the buckwheat flour and hot water. Mix until it becomes a thick paste.

2. Add the remaining ingredients. As the dough thickens, begin to knead it by hand until it becomes non-sticky.

3. Divide the dough into 12 balls. Roll the balls between two sheets of parchment as thin as possible into circular tortillas. If at any point tortillas are sticky, add additional buckwheat or rice flour. Optional: Cut each tortilla into a perfectly round shape using the top of a bowl.

4. Place tortillas one at a time in skillet. Lightly brush each side with a little oil. Cook over medium heat for 1 minute on each side. You will know they are done when air bubbles have begun to form. Remove from skillet and repeat until all 12 tortillas are made.

Note: If you are able to tolerate soy, we found that non-stick spray worked great for this. For the best texture, always serve these tortillas warm. This can be done by briefly heating in the microwave or skillet.

INGREDIENTS:

248 grams buckwheat flour (2 lightly filled cups)

1½ cups boiling water

240 grams tapioca starch (2 cups)

65 grams brown rice flour (½ lightly filled cup)

1½ teaspoons xanthan gum

1¼ teaspoons salt

Buckwheat Molasses Bread

....

The outside of this bread is crispy while the inside is soft and chewy. We like to serve it with jam, but some of our friends enjoy eating it with their Thanksgiving turkey and cranberry sauce.

Yield: One 9 x 5 inch loaf

DIRECTIONS:

1. Preheat oven to 375 degrees F. Oil a 9 x 5 inch bread pan. In a small bowl, pour boiling water over flax seed meal, psyllium husks, and prunes. Let sit for 10 minutes.

2. In a medium-sized bowl, whisk together the buckwheat flour, tapioca starch, baking powder, and salt.

3. Once the prunes have softened for 10 minutes, puree the mixture in a food processor for about 1 minute. One at a time, add the molasses, oil, and 4 egg yolks (put the egg whites in a large mixing bowl and set aside). Puree until smooth (a few very small bits of prunes left are okay; they'll add texture to the bread). Set aside.

4. With an electric beater, beat the egg whites in the large bowl until soft peaks form. Beat in the prune mixture on medium speed, then the dry ingredients. Add 2 tablespoons of water. Continue beating until completely mixed.

5. Pour the batter into the bread pan. Wet your hands and smooth down the top of the bread (you'll probably have to wet your hands a few times). If desired for appearance, score the top of the bread in three strokes very lightly with a sharp knife.

6. Bake for 30 minutes, then put aluminum foil over the top to keep it from browning too much, and bake another 30 minutes, or until a knife inserted in the middle comes out clean.

7. Remove from the oven, allow to sit for 5 minutes, then turn onto a cooling rack. You might need to use a knife to separate the sides of the bread from the pan, but it should come out pretty easily. Let cool completely before cutting.

Store in an airtight container at room temperature or freeze for later use.

INGREDIENTS:

¼ cup ground flax seed meal

¼ cup whole psyllium husks (ground chia seeds will not work)

1½ cups pitted prunes

¾ cup boiling water

124 grams buckwheat flour (1 lightly filled cup)

120 grams tapioca starch (1 cup)

4 teaspoons double acting baking powder

¾ teaspoon salt

¼ cup molasses

2 tablespoons plus 2 teaspoons mild flavored oil

4 large eggs, separated and at room temperature

2 tablespoons water

German Chocolate Cookie Sandwiches

· ·

This modern twist on the classic cake makes use of buckwheat's dense texture to create a dark chocolate cookie that will delight your senses. This was a favorite among our recipe testers.

Yield: One dozen cookie sandwiches

Directions:

1. In a large bowl, combine the butter, sugar and cream. Add the eggs and vanilla and beat to mix.

2. Add remaining cookie Ingredients: buckwheat flour, tapioca starch, cocoa powder, baking powder and salt. Mix until dough comes together.

3. Place the dough in the fridge for about an hour so that it becomes easier to handle.

4. Preheat oven to 350 degrees F.

5. Roll heaping tablespoon sized balls of dough into your hands and flatten slightly. Place a few inches apart on an ungreased cookie sheet. The cookies will spread as they bake.

6. Bake 14-15 minutes.

7. Remove from oven and allow to cool. Make the cookies into sandwiches by filling them with the German Chocolate Cake Frosting or another favorite frosting of choice.

Note: Whenever we make these cookies with unrefined granulated sugar (palm sugar, Sucanat or turbinado), we like to run it through a coffee mill to powder it slightly. We find we have better results.

Ingredients:

1 cup butter, softened

1½ cup granulated sugar

2 Eggs

2 teaspoons pure vanilla extract

125 grams buckwheat flour (1 lightly filled cup)

120 grams tapioca starch (1 cup)

70 grams unsweetened cocoa powder (⅔ cup)

¾ teaspoon double acting baking powder

½ teaspoon salt

Frosting

See frosting section for German Chocolate Cake Frosting

Chocolate-Coated Apricot Brownie Bites

. . . .

These brownie bites make an elegant dessert. A rich and dense brownie ball is covered with a layer of chocolate, then cooled in the fridge for the perfect bite-sized treat. Make sure you have room in your fridge for them.

Yield: Four dozen brownie bites

Directions:

1. Preheat the oven to 350 degrees F. Grease four 12-cup mini-muffin tins.

2. Blend the apricots and coconut milk in a blender for about 30 seconds, just until the apricots are chopped but not completely pureed. Pour into a large mixing bowl and stir in the applesauce, sugar, and vanilla extract.

3. In a medium-sized bowl, whisk together the buckwheat flour, tapioca starch, cocoa, baking powder, and salt. Stir the dry ingredients into the wet until completely mixed.

4. Scoop the batter into the muffin tins about halfway Dip your fingers in water and use them to spread the batter evenly. Bake for 14 minutes. Remove to a cooling rack.

5. Once the brownie bites have cooled, heat coconut milk in a small pan over low heat. Stir in maple syrup and vanilla extract for a minute. Add chocolate and stir until smooth. Dip brownies in chocolate completely, shaking a bit to get excess chocolate off when you take them out. Place on wax or parchment paper.

6. Once you've dipped all of the brownies, top them with chopped apricots and place in the fridge to chill. This only takes about ten minutes. Once you can touch the coating without it sticking completely to your fingers, you're golden!

Store in an airtight container in the fridge or freeze for later use.

Ingredients:

Brownies

1½ cups dried apricots

¾ cup full-fat canned coconut milk

¾ cup unsweetened applesauce

¾ cup unrefined granulated sugar

1 teaspoon pure vanilla extract

132 grams buckwheat flour (1 lightly filled cup plus 1 tablespoon)

60 grams tapioca starch (½ cup)

40 grams unsweetened cocoa powder (½ lightly filled cup)

2 teaspoons baking powder

¾ teaspoon salt

Chocolate Coating

½ cup full-fat canned coconut milk

6 tablespoons maple syrup

1 teaspoon pure vanilla extract

4 ounces unsweetened chocolate, chopped

3 dried apricots, finely chopped

Sesame Buckwheat Breakfast Cookies

· ·

These are a light breakfast cookie, perfect for eating with your morning yogurt and fruit. We've included instructions for making them egg-free, too.

Yield: Two dozen cookies

Directions:

1. Preheat the oven to 350 degrees F. Lightly grease 2 cookie sheets.

2. In a large bowl, whisk together the buckwheat flour, tapioca starch, sesame seeds, baking powder, salt, cinnamon, and xanthan gum.

3. In a medium-sized bowl, whisk together the sugar, egg, vanilla, oil, and applesauce. Pour the wet ingredients into the dry, stirring until completely mixed.

4. Drop by the heaping tablespoon onto a greased cookie sheet, 12 to a sheet. Wet your fingertips and use them to flatten the cookies into discs, about ½ inch tall. Bake for 12 minutes.

5. Let cool for a few minutes on the cookie sheet before removing to a cooling rack.

To make egg free: Add 4 tablespoons of applesauce for a total of 6 tablespoons. Add 1 teaspoon of baking powder for a total of 3 teaspoons.

Store in an airtight container at room temperature or freeze for later use.

Ingredients:

124 grams buckwheat flour (1 lightly filled cup)

40 grams tapioca starch (⅓ cup)

⅔ cup sesame seeds

2 teaspoons baking powder

½ teaspoon salt

½ teaspoon cinnamon

¼ teaspoon xanthan gum

⅔ cup unrefined granulated sugar

1 large egg

1 tablespoon pure vanilla extract

6 tablespoons mild flavored oil

2 tablespoons unsweetened applesauce

Winter Spice Pancakes

Who doesn't love waking up to the smell of pancakes? With this recipe, you get the double power of pancakes with the warm aroma of gingerbread spices. Thick and fluffy, you'll find your whole family will go back for seconds.

Yield: One dozen pancakes

DIRECTIONS:

1. In a large bowl, whisk together the buckwheat flour, potato starch, baking powder, sugar, salt, cinnamon, nutmeg, ginger, and cloves.

2. In a medium-sized bowl, whisk applesauce, oil, molasses, and 1 cup milk vigorously for a good 60 seconds. Make a well in the center of the dry ingredients and pour wet into dry, whisking continuously until batter is smooth. Add more milk by the tablespoon if needed.

3. Heat oil or butter alternative in a pan over medium heat. Scoop about ¼ cup batter per pancake and let cook a little less than 2 minutes per side. Watch for bubbles to appear around the edges, which will let you know the pancake is ready to be flipped.

Freeze leftover pancakes for an easy breakfast in the morning.

INGREDIENTS:

155 grams buckwheat flour (1¼ lightly filled cups)

86 grams potato starch (½ cup)

2 teaspoons baking powder

2 teaspoons unrefined granulated sugar

½ teaspoon salt

½ teaspoon ground cinnamon

¼ teaspoon ground nutmeg

¼ teaspoon ground ginger

⅛ teaspoon ground cloves

¼ cup unsweetened applesauce

2 tablespoons mild flavored oil

2 tablespoons molasses

1 cup milk (plus an extra ¼ cup if needed)

62 grams buckwheat flour (½ lightly filled cup)

78 grams white rice flour (½ lightly filled cup)

60 grams tapioca starch (½ cup)

½ teaspoon salt

1 teaspoon double acting baking powder

½ cup granulated sugar

1 tablespoon pure vanilla extract

½ cup + 2 tablespoons milk

2 apples sliced into wedges

1½ teaspoons cinnamon

¼ cup granulated sugar

2 tablespoons melted butter or oil

Apple Kuchen

....

This classic recipe is pretty to look at and easy to make! This kuchen tastes its best when made with light buckwheat flour.

Yield: One 8-inch cake

DIRECTIONS:

1. Preheat oven to 375 degrees F.

2. Combine and beat together all the buckwheat flour, white rice flour, tapioca starch, salt, baking powder, sugar, vanilla extract, and milk.

2. Pour the batter into a greased cake pan (8-9 inch).

3. Slice the apples into wedges. Mix them in a bowl with the cinnamon and granulated sugar.

4. Gently press the apples in a circular fan-like pattern into the prepared batter. Allow for the majority of the apple surface to remain visible.

5. Brush the top of the kuchen with 2 tablespoons of the melted butter or oil.

6. Bake 33-35 minutes.

    Slice and serve warm.

Ask the Expert

. . . .

Nicole Hunn, the author of *Gluten-Free on a Shoestring: 125 Easy Recipes for Eating Well on the Cheap* teaches her readers that eating gluten-free doesn't have to be expensive. With beautiful photography and a sense of humor, she also shares recipes like her Ciabatta Bread and Cream Wafers at her blog, www.glutenfreeonashoestring.com.

How long have you been baking gluten-free? I've been baking gluten-free since 2004. Bette Hagman's books were a lifeline for me back once I discovered them in early 2005. She taught me to have greater expectations of gluten-free food.

Do you remember the first thing you ever baked gluten-free? I vividly recall making vanilla cupcakes from a mix for my son's first birthday. It was the mix that someone on the Internet had recommended as "the best." They turned out so crumbly that I had to vacuum the floor, the table—and the children. Not only were the cupcakes bone dry, they tasted unpleasant. After I vacuumed the children, I cried. It was early February 2005.

Do you ever use commercial gluten-free all-purpose mixes? I use Better Batter All-Purpose Gluten-Free Flour almost exclusively in my recipes. When I first started baking gluten-free from scratch, I followed Bette Hagman's flour blend guidelines and recipes.

Not long after I started blogging, some of my readers recommended Better Batter to me. I tried it and never looked back. It is the only commercially available blend I have tried that works in everything from cakes and cookies to yeast breads—and everything tastes as it should. Better Batter is also fairly priced, and is very affordable in the 25-pound bags. I like the simplicity and normalcy of using a commercially prepared blend. I also find that it has the fewest barriers to entry into gluten-free baking. But all of my recipes can be made with any true all-purpose gluten-free flour, Better Batter or otherwise.

What are the top three things every new baker should know?

1. You should not have to compromise to eat gluten-free. Gluten-free baked goods should taste as good as conventional foods. Keep those standards high.

2. If a mix fails, it's not your fault.

3. Start out by using someone else's tried and true recipes, not by creating your own. Follow the directions to the letter. Walk before you run. Gluten-free baking isn't hard if you have a good recipe.

Do you have any money saving tips for gluten-free bakers? Moneysaving is sort of my stock in trade in *Gluten-Free on a Shoestring*, so I'd better have some tips! The most important tip is to bake from scratch whenever you can, but keep it simple so you're not spending all day in the kitchen. The more processed your ingredients are, the more you're going to pay for them. Take advantage of what is in season, and buy fresh produce that is, in fact, fresh. If the ingredients go bad before you are able to use them, that's not a good value. I also like to do what I call "piggybacking" one meal on another. Make double the amount of one basic component of a meal, and use it in two different ways that week. For example, make a double batch of cornbread. Use one batch to serve alongside chili for a hearty, winters meal, and let the other batch dry out on the counter and use it to make cornbread stuffing a couple nights later.

What tips would you give for someone wanting to convert a family favorite recipe to gluten-free? Follow a recipe created by someone who develops gluten-free recipes for a living for something in the same category as the family recipe you'd like to convert. So if it's a cake you're looking to convert, make a few gluten-free cakes first from tried and true gluten-free recipes. Get a feel for how to expect the batter to appear and behave. And if at first you don't succeed, try again.

What are your favorite flours to work with and why? Other than an all-purpose gluten-free flour blend, I love working with corn flours. Masa harina is versatile and forgiving for making everything from arepas and pupusas to fresh corn tortillas. Once you've eaten one of those you'll never go back to the store-bought kind. Coarsely ground cornmeal is another favorite, as it's great for making hearty cornbread and corn muffins.

I also love polenta for getting a quick weeknight dinner on the table.

What are your three favorite types of recipes to bake and why? I love making gluten-free breads—both with and without yeast. It's amazing how close you can come in texture to the yeasted version and still get these favorites done in record time. But my first baking love is yeast breads, especially shaped yeast breads like rolls and breadsticks. Beyond that, I love baking clones of nostalgic foods, like Nilla Wafers and Ritz Crackers. It's easy to assume that, when you're gluten-free, you have to close that chapter in your life. It's rewarding to show people that nothing is out of reach, and that you should nurture that nostalgia rather than snuffing it out.

What kind of recipes would you suggest for a beginner to start with? Drop cookies are reliable. They require little handling, and converting most drop cookie recipes is a breeze. The most important thing is to be successful early on in your baking life. Success breeds confidence, which leads to more willingness to take chances.

What's the most challenging recipe you ever developed and why? My recipe for White Sandwich Bread was the most challenging for me. It was the first successful gluten-free yeast bread recipe I developed from the ground up. I had to reinvent the wheel, or so it seemed to me at the time. I read everything I could find about the general characteristics of gluten-free flours as compared to gluten-containing flours, and the role of stabilizers in successful gluten-free bread baking. And I was still lost. I lost count of the number of fails at some point, but I'll never forget that feeling of success.

Do you bake by weight or volume? I bake by weight. For a long time, my recipes were written with volume measurements only because I didn't want to be too prescriptive—and I know that most Americans are only comfortable measuring by volume. I was doing it by weight at home, but I knew the corresponding volume measurements. It took me an embarrassingly long time to realize that I could just include both measurements—weight and volume, where appropriate—and let my readers make their own choices.

Can you give our readers some bread making tips? Are there certain flours or other ingredients that you always use when making bread? I almost always use some cream of tartar and apple cider vinegar as stabilizers. I use egg whites and/or whole eggs, depending upon the recipe and how I want it to look and taste. Using milk as liquid rather than water tends to yield a more tender crumb.

Do you have any tips on how to make gluten-free bread without the use of yeast? If you're not using yeast to make bread, you will most likely need some sort of chemical leavener in the form of baking soda and/or baking powder. Make sure you use aluminum-free double-acting baking powder. Double acting means that it is activated once

by the addition of liquid, and again by the heat of the oven. Baking soda is often used in smaller amounts to balance out the acidity of ingredients such as natural cocoa powder and honey.

Is there anything else you think our readers should know about gluten-free baking? Have high standards make demands on the marketplace. Gluten-free doesn't mean taste free. Any company that tries to sell you poor quality gluten-free ingredients for a steep price should find itself out of business in a hurry. We deserve better.

Chapter 4

Teff Flour

We're pleased to introduce you to a whole grain flour that acts, in many ways, as a white flour does. Teff flour contains twice the protein content of rice flour and offers structure to baked goods. It is a soft flour that gives your baked goods a light, soft, fluffy and airy texture. But that's not all: while these baked goods are soft on the inside, they also have a delicious crust. This crust will range in texture depending on the moisture and fat content of the baked good. Take, for example, our Gingerbread Men recipe. They are soft on the inside and have the perfect amount of exterior crunch. Teff is mildly sweet and will add moisture to your baked goods.

Nutritional Highlights:

Teff, the smallest grain in the world, is known for its easy digestibility and excellent amino acid composition. Its high lysine content aids the body's absorption of calcium and its high iron content is thought to be beneficial for those looking to increase their iron intake.

Brand Comparison:

Teff comes in two colors: dark brown and ivory. The darker variety has a nuttier taste, one that complements warm spices. We used the darker variety for the development of these recipes because it's much more accessible. Ivory has a lighter flavor, and could be used in an even larger range of recipes, as its flavor will play less of a role in the taste of the baked good.

We have found that brand *does* make a difference in the overall results of most recipes. The brands we prefer are:

- **Dakota Prairie**
- **Nuts.com**
- **Bob's Red Mill**

Best Flours to Substitute for Teff Flour:

We don't recommend making substitutions with teff flour recipes unless it's in small percentages. Due to teff's very unique texture and flavor, desired results via substitution will vary. Substituting another flour can work but the taste, texture and moisture content will change. Here are the best substitutes for teff flour:

Buckwheat Flour: Use this only as a substitution in recipes that can be dense, like our Oat Bars or Toasted Pine Nut & Rosemary Shortbread. Try subbing in buckwheat flour in a 1:1 ratio. Buckwheat and teff both have flavors that work well with the same spices and sweeteners (molasses, pumpkin pie spices), but buckwheat is a much heavier flour.

Sorghum, Garbanzo Bean, Millet, and Quinoa flour: These all have good structure in baked goods (that is, they rise well and in most cases do not collapse). But they are heavier than teff and are only recommended as a last resort. When subbing flours keep in mind that both texture and flavor will be altered.

Teff Flour Tips:

- Teff's flavor tastes phenomenal with spices such as chocolate, nutmeg, cinnamon, or cloves.

- Teff flour is very light and is a great choice in egg-free baking.

- Teff has a distinct crunchy texture not seen in other gluten-free flours. For this reason, we love it in cookie or bread recipes to add a nice crust.

- Teff can work wonderfully in pastry applications. It's perfect for pie crust.

- Dark teff gives its baked goods a dark rich color.

Fun Uses for Teff Flour

- Teff in its whole grain form can be cooked like rice and makes delicious porridge.
- Teff flour can be added to thicken soups/stews or to make gravy.

Whole Grain Dinner Rolls (Egg-Free)

. . . .

Enjoy soft and chewy rolls that will remind you of restaurant bread basket rolls. Although these are egg-free, they rise beautifully and are easy to make. Remember to first read our how-to section on making a steam box for your dough to rise in.

Yield: 18 rolls or 4 mini loaves

Directions:

1. In a medium-sized bowl, whisk together the teff flour, brown rice flour, potato starch, baking powder, sugar, and salt. Set aside.

2. In a small bowl, stir the yeast and 1 teaspoon of sugar into the water. Let sit for 5 minutes to proof. The yeast on the top should begin to foam so you know the yeast is active.

3. In a large bowl, stir together the psyllium husks, applesauce, and oil. Let sit until the yeast is done proofing, then pour the yeast and water into the psyllium mixture.

4. Beat on medium for about 30 seconds, then add the dry ingredients slowly. Continue to beat on medium speed for 5 minutes.

5. Shape the dough into a ball. Place in a bowl and brush the top with oil. Place in your steam box for 30 minutes.

6. After the dough has risen, preheat the oven to 375 degrees F. Break the dough into 18 balls (about ¼ cup each), rolling each in your palm to make it smooth. Alternatively, you can make four mini loaves.

7. Place on a greased cookie sheet and bake for 22 minutes. Serve hot.

Store in an airtight container in the freezer for later use.

Ingredients:

- 232 grams teff flour (1½ lightly filled cups)
- 162 grams brown rice flour (1¼ lightly filled cups)
- 172 grams potato starch (1 cup)
- 4 teaspoons baking powder
- ¼ cup unrefined granulated sugar
- 1 teaspoon salt
- 2 cups lukewarm water
- 2¼ teaspoons quick rise yeast
- 1 teaspoon unrefined granulated sugar
- 6 tablespoons psyllium whole husks
- ⅓ cup unsweetened applesauce
- ⅓ cup mild flavored oil plus extra for brushing on top

Pizza Roll Ups

This crust is soft, chewy and pliable, perfect for a pizza roll up! Teff is an unusual flour to use in pizza crust, but in this instance, it makes all the difference. We tried this recipe with various types of flour, and the teff was by far the favorite! Add in your favorite pizza toppings and enjoy with a side salad for a simple dinner.

Yield: Two hearty or 4 small servings

DIRECTIONS:

1. Preheat the oven to 400 degrees F.

2. Pour boiling water over flax seed meal and psyllium husks in a small bowl. Set aside.

3. Proof the yeast by stirring the yeast and honey into the warm water. Set aside for 5 minutes while you're preparing the rest of the ingredients. The yeast should bubble up and increase in size.

4. Whisk the teff flour, tapioca starch, potato starch, baking powder, salt, and oregano together in a large bowl.

5. With an electric beater, beat the egg white in a large bowl until soft peaks form. Beat in the flax seed mixture, yeast mixture, apple cider vinegar, and olive oil. Slowly add in the dry ingredients, continuing to beat for five minutes on medium speed.

6. Lightly oil a cookie sheet and pour your batter onto it. It will be the consistency of thick pancake batter. Spread the batter into a rectangle about 10 x 14 inches (¼ inch thick). Put in the oven and bake for 10 minutes.

7. Remove from oven and use a spatula to separate the bread from the pan. Thinly spread pizza sauce and any toppings on it. Roll the bread up, making sure to put it seam side down on the pan. Put back in the oven for 10-15 minutes. Serve hot.

Best when eaten hot. Store leftovers in an airtight container in the fridge or frozen for later use.

INGREDIENTS:

1 tablespoon ground flax seed meal

1 tablespoon whole psyllium husks

6 tablespoons boiling water

½ cup warm water

2 teaspoons honey

2 ¼ teaspoons quick rise yeast

77 grams teff flour (½ lightly filled cup)

60 grams tapioca starch (½ cup)

43 grams potato starch (¼ cup)

1 tablespoon double acting baking powder

¾ teaspoon salt

½ teaspoon dried oregano

1 egg white, room temperature

1 teaspoon apple cider vinegar

1½ tablespoons olive oil

Your favorite pizza sauce and toppings

Gingerbread Men

. . . .

These cookies show off the classic texture that teff flour provides to its recipes, soft on the inside with a slightly crunchy texture on the surface. This is a special recipe, adapted from Mom's version, a childhood staple. We hope it creates many happy memories for your family.

Yield: Three dozen cookies

Directions:

1. Make the powdered sugar by running Sucanat or palm sugar through a blender or a coffee grinder.

2. In a bowl, mix the shortening, molasses, powdered sugar and water using an electric mixer.

3. Add the remaining ingredients. The dough will be very thick.

4. Cover two cookie sheets with parchment and preheat oven to 350 degrees F.

5. Lightly dust a clean countertop with some teff flour. Roll the dough out ¼- ½ inch thick, dusting with more flour as needed to prevent sticking. Cut with cookie cutter and place on prepared cookie sheet.

6. Bake 7-9 minutes. Seven minutes yields a softer cookie while nine minutes yields a crispier cookie.

7. Allow the cookies to cool before transporting.

Store in a sealed bag at room temperature or freeze for another day.

Ingredients:

5 tablespoons shortening

224 grams molasses (¾ cup)

96 grams powdered Sucanat or palm sugar

3 tablespoons water

250 grams teff flour (1½ packed cups)

146 grams superfine white rice flour (1¼ packed cups)

94 grams tapioca starch (¾ cup)

1½ teaspoons baking soda

¾ teaspoon salt

1 tablespoon powdered ginger

½ teaspoon cloves

1 teaspoon cinnamon

¼ teaspoon xanthan gum

Oat Bars

* *

Like granola bars, you can make these any flavor you like: chocolate chip, raisin, coconut, almond, etc.

Yield: 16 bars

Directions:

1. Preheat the oven to 350 degrees F. Grease an 8 x 8 inch glass baking dish.

2. In a medium-sized bowl, whisk together the oats, teff flour, tapioca starch, and salt. Set aside.

3. Stir the boiling water into the chia and flax to make slurry in a small bowl. Set aside for about 5 minutes.

4. In a large bowl, cream the coconut oil with the sugar, applesauce, and vanilla. Small chunks are okay, as they will melt a bit when you add the hot flax/chia slurry.

5. Stir the chia/flax mixture into the coconut oil until well blended. Stir in the flour a little at a time until completely combined. Stir in your mixings of choice. Scoop into baking dish and press evenly.

6. Bake for 45 minutes. Serve warm or room temperature. The bars will crisp up as they cool.

Note: Toast oats in a dry skillet over medium-low heat, shaking often to ensure even browning. Once the oats become fragrant and very lightly browned, take them out of the pan.

Store in an airtight container at room temperature.

Ingredients:

- 101 grams certified gluten-free rolled oats (1 cup)
- 77 grams teff flour (½ lightly filled cup)
- 60 grams tapioca starch (½ cup)
- ½ teaspoon salt
- 1 tablespoon ground chia seeds
- 1 tablespoon ground flax seed meal
- 6 tablespoons boiling water
- ½ cup coconut oil
- ¼ cup plus 2 tablespoons unrefined granulated sugar
- 2 tablespoons unsweetened applesauce
- ½ teaspoon pure vanilla extract
- ¾ cup total of your choice: coconut flakes, chopped dried fruit, raisins, chocolate chips, nuts, etc.

Toasted Pine Nut & Rosemary Flatbread Crisps

∙∙∙

This is one of our most unique recipes. The goal wasn't to recreate a classic recipe, but rather to have fun with teff, one of our favorite flours. The resulting recipe is both savory and sweet, and it's a delicious complement to a wine and cheese platter.

Yield: 16 squares

Directions:

1. Preheat the oven to 350 degrees F. Set aside an 8 x 8 inch baking dish.

2. Stir the boiling water into the flax and chia in a small bowl. Set aside.

3. Whisk together the teff flour, tapioca starch, potato starch, ¼ teaspoon of sea salt, pine nuts, and rosemary in a medium bowl. Set aside.

4. In a large bowl, cream the shortening with the sugar and vanilla extract. Stir in the flax/chia slurry until well combined. Stir in the flour mixture until well combined. Press into the baking pan and sprinkle the top lightly with sea salt (⅛ teaspoon or less).

5. Bake for 50 minutes or until edges begin o darken slightly. Let cool completely before cutting into squares.

Note: Toast pine nuts in a dry skillet over medium-low heat, shaking often to ensure even browning. Once the pine nuts become fragrant and lightly browned, take them out of the pan.

Best when served on day one. Store leftovers in an airtight container at room temperature.

Ingredients:

- 1 tablespoon ground flax seed meal
- 1 tablespoon ground chia seeds
- 6 tablespoons boiling water
- 106 grams teff flour (½ lightly filled cup plus 3 tablespoons)
- 30 grams tapioca starch (¼ cup)
- 43 grams potato starch (¼ cup)
- ¼ teaspoon fine grain sea salt plus a dash extra for sprinkling on top
- ¼ cup pine nuts, lightly toasted and coarsely chopped
- 1 teaspoon minced fresh rosemary (recommended) or ½ teaspoon dried rosemary
- 7 tablespoons shortening
- ¼ cup plus 2 tablespoons unrefined granulated sugar
- ½ teaspoon pure vanilla extract

Cranberry Upside Down Cake

This moist cake is sweetened with a tart cranberry glaze. Serve it warm with ice cream for dessert or on its own with your afternoon tea.

Yield: One 8 x 8 inch cake

Directions:

1. Preheat the oven to 350 degrees F. Line the bottom of an 8 x 8 inch or 9 inch round baking dish with parchment paper. Pour cranberries in and coat evenly with ¼ cup of honey and 1 teaspoon of cinnamon. Set aside.

2. In a medium-sized bowl, whisk the teff flour, tapioca starch, potato starch, baking powder, baking soda, and salt. Set aside.

3. Stir together flax seed meal, psyllium husks and boiling water in a small bowl and set aside.

4. In a large bowl, beat the shortening, honey, applesauce, and vanilla extract for three minutes on medium speed. Beat in the flax seed mix, then beat in the dry ingredients and milk, alternating between the two until a smooth batter is formed.

5. Pour the batter over the cranberries and bake for 45 minutes or until a toothpick inserted in the middle comes out clean.

6. Remove from oven and let sit in dish for about 5 minutes. Use a knife to separate the edges from the pan, then turn over gently onto a plate. If it doesn't come out right away, tap on the bottom of the pan to help it along.

Serve warm or room temperature. Best eaten the first day although leftovers can be stored in an airtight container in the fridge or frozen for later use.

Ingredients:

- 2 cups fresh cranberries
- ¼ cup honey
- 1 teaspoon cinnamon
- 1 tablespoon ground flax seed meal
- 1 teaspoon whole psyllium husks or ground chia seeds
- 3 tablespoons boiling water
- 155 grams teff flour (1 lightly filled cup)
- 60 grams tapioca starch (½ cup)
- 43 grams potato starch (¼ cup)
- 1 tablespoon baking powder
- ½ teaspoon baking soda
- ½ teaspoon salt
- ½ cup shortening
- ¾ cup honey
- 3 tablespoons unsweetened applesauce
- 2 teaspoons pure vanilla extract
- ½ cup milk

Oreo-Style Cookies

Teff provides a crunchy texture to these delicious cookies. For variation, try using different extracts in the filling to change the flavor. Peppermint cookies are always a hit during the winter holiday season. We always keep a bag of unfrosted cookies in the freezer to use as the crust for pies and cheesecakes.

Yield: Two dozen cookies

Directions:

1. Preheat oven to 375 degrees F.

2. Beat and cream the butter, vanilla extract and sugar. Add in the water, salt and baking powder.

3. Start adding the flours, starches and cocoa powder a little at a time, mixing on high. The dough will be really thick, almost like Play-Doh.

4. Roll dough out in between 2 sheets of parchment to about ⅛ inch thick. Using a small, circular cookie cutter, cut all of the dough. Place on 1-2 large cookie sheets covered in parchment.

5. Bake 10 minutes. Cookies will harden as they cool.

6. While the cookies are cooling, make the frosting by combining all the ingredients using a hand mixer. Spoon or pipe frosting onto half the cookies. Top and sandwich the cookies together.

Notes: Be sure to roll out and cut the dough right away, or cover it until you are using it. Because the recipe contains so little liquid the dough is prone to drying out and then will become hard to work with.

This recipe works best made in a stand mixer. The dough is on the dry side and needs the extra mixing. In order for these cookies to have the best texture we recommend running your granulated sugar of choice briefly through a coffee grinder or in your blender until powdered.

Ingredients:

- 5 tablespoons softened butter or shortening
- 2 teaspoons pure vanilla extract
- 1 cup powdered, unrefined granulated sugar
- 5 tablespoons water
- ¼ teaspoon salt
- ½ teaspoon double acting baking powder
- 155 grams tapioca starch (1¼ cup)
- 75 grams teff flour (½ lightly filled cup)
- 60 grams brown or white rice flour (½ lightly filled cup)
- 60 grams unsweetened cocoa powder (¾ lightly filled cup)

Filling

- 4 tablespoons softened butter
- 2 tablespoons milk
- ¾ cup shortening
- 4½ cups powdered sugar
- 1 tablespoon tapioca or arrowroot starch
- 1 teaspoon pure vanilla extract

Gingerbread Angel Food Cake

Our wintry take on this classic dessert is a special one. The gingerbread spice takes this perfectly textured cake over the top. We suggest serving it with a chocolate sauce and coconut whipped cream. Looking to make an angel food cake without the spices? This recipe works fantastic that way too.

Yield: One cake

READ THESE **10** QUICK TIPS BEFORE YOU BEGIN THE RECIPE TO ASSURE YOU GET ONLY THE BEST RESULTS!

1. This cake must be baked in a grease-free pan. Make sure also that you are not using a pan that has a non-stick surface. The cake needs to stick to the pan.

2. An undercooked cake will fall. Bake it the full time.

3. Make sure to incorporate the flour well into the egg foam.

4. Sifting the flours together makes a big difference. You want the flours perfectly blended.

5. The eggs need to be at room temperature before you whip them.

6. Do not open the oven during the cooking time. Not even once. This could make your cake fall.

7. Bake the cake on the lowest rack in your oven.

8. Gently remove the cake from the oven and allow it to cool completely before removing it from the pan. We suggest flipping the pan upside down and letting it cool that way.

9. Use a serrated knife when it comes time to cut and serve the cake; this will allow it to remain fluffy.

10. Follow the directions in the order they are given. This will ensure perfect results every time.

DIRECTIONS:

1. Remove your eggs from the refrigerator and allow them to sit on the counter until they come to room temperature.

2. Sift together the teff flour, tapioca starch, potato starch, sugar, xanthan gum, and spices. Set aside.

3. Separate the egg whites from the yolks. Place the egg whites in a stainless steel bowl; discard the yolks.

INGREDIENTS:

116 grams teff flour (¾ lightly filled cup)

90 grams tapioca or arrowroot starch (¾ cup)

50 grams potato starch (¼ cup)

1 cup organic cane sugar

1 teaspoon xanthan gum

2 teaspoons cinnamon

2¾ teaspoons ground ginger

½ teaspoon ground allspice

¼ teaspoon ground cloves

12 egg whites at room temperature

¼ teaspoon salt

1¼ teaspoon cream of tarter

1¼ cup powdered cane sugar

4. Preheat the oven to 325 degrees F and make sure that your oven rack is at its lowest point.

5. Double check to see if the whites are at room temperature. If they are, add the salt and begin whipping. Once the egg whites are foamy, add the cream of tartar. Whip more.

6. Once soft peaks begin to form you may start adding the cane sugar. Do this a little at a time until you have added all of the sugar.

7. Beat until stiff peaks form.

8. Using a spatula, gently fold in the flour mixture a little at a time. The key here is gentle movements so that you do not destroy the peaks. It's crucial that the flour is mixed in thoroughly. Your peaks are going to lose a little bit of their volume while you do this. That's expected.

9. Place the fully incorporated mixture into your ungreased angel food cake pan. Using your spatula, smooth out the top.

10. Place the cake into the oven and bake for 1 hour and 10 minutes.

11. Gently remove the cake from the oven and allow it to cool upside down for at least 1 hour.

12. To remove the cake, run a sharp knife around the edge of the cake and flip it onto a serving platter.

Note: This recipe uses both cane and powdered cane sugar, cane for the flour mix and powdered for the egg whites. Make powdered cane sugar by running it through a mini food processor or coffee mill. Regular white powdered sugar also works well.

Ask the Expert

Once bakery owner and former Founding Editor-in-Chief of *Rachael Ray Magazine,* Silvana Nardone knows a thing or two about baking. When her son received the diagnosis of gluten intolerant, her world was turned upside down. This challenge inspired the creation of her best-selling book *Cooking For Isaiah: Gluten-Free & Dairy Free Recipes for Easy Delicious Meals.* We hope you enjoy Silvana's tips!

How long have you been baking gluten-free? The day before Halloween 2007, my now 15-year-old son Isaiah was diagnosed with gluten and dairy intolerance. The next day, we trick-o-treated as planned and then we went cold turkey.

Do you remember the first thing you ever baked gluten-free? How did it turn out? The first thing I baked was cornbread. When the doctor told us that Isaiah couldn't eat gluten, I asked him what he would miss the most. His answer was cornbread. I thought I got off the hook since cornbread traditionally calls for half cornmeal and half flour. Oh, how I was wrong. It took me three tries, then I nailed the perfect gluten-free, dairy-free cornbread—moist, flavorful and with a deliciously buttery texture. The recipe is in *Cooking for Isaiah.*

Do you ever use commercial gluten-free all-purpose mixes? My approach to gluten-free baking and cooking is to recreate my kids' favorite foods. To that end, we prefer the mix I developed, Silvana's Gluten-Free All-Purpose Flour Blend. Through the years, what I have found is that some store-bought brands use added sweeteners or ingredients that yield undesirable textures or flavors.

What should every new gluten-free baker know? Brands matter. Finding the tapioca flour from Shiloh Farms was a game changer: it was the only one that didn't leave a metallic aftertaste. Also, if you're developing recipes from scratch, expect failure but don't accept defeat. Especially in the beginning, you have to feel your way around a recipe, but with perseverance, you'll get it right.

What are your favorite types of recipes to bake and why? I enjoy baking anything that puts a smile on my children's faces! In our house, this usually means cookies, cupcakes and biscuits.

What kind of recipes would you suggest for a beginner to start with? Make something you really miss eating. It will be challenging, but your determination will ultimately yield tremendous satisfaction.

Chapter 5

Sweet White Rice Flour

. . . .

a.k.a. Glutinous Rice Flour or Mochiko

Sweet rice flour is often misunderstood and therefore underused. We hope to change that. Sweet rice flour is an absolute superstar for cake and pastry recipes. It far exceeds many others in its ability to make heavenly cookies, fluffy cakes, puff pastry, pie crust, doughnuts, and more. We love this flour so much that we had a hard time stopping at just ten recipes.

Sweet rice flour is made from Asian sticky rice. Just like the rice, the flour is sticky and is able to hold together well in baking applications. Your days of crumbly baked goods have come to an end with this flour. This stickiness works perfectly to hold dough together. For example, our Pate Brisee will transfer right into the pie dish without any issues. In the past, gluten-free pie crusts were known for their inability to hold together enough to do this. We recommend sweet rice flour for cake recipes. Cakes using this flour have a wonderful soft and fluffy texture. Try the Double Chocolate Chip Cake, Lemon Bars and Cinnamon Rolls. You'll be a sweet rice flour-convert after one bite.

Nutritional Highlights:

Sweet white rice flour is high in starch and not as nutritious as many of the other flours in our books. Foods using sweet white rice flour should be eaten in moderation.

Brand Comparison:

Almost all brands use a finely ground sweet white rice flour that makes it easy to achieve a perfectly smooth texture. We suggest buying your sweet rice flour from an Asian grocery store where it is labeled Glutinous Rice Flour. Do not be concerned about the name, we assure you it's gluten-free!

We tested several brands and these were our favorites:

- **Dakota Prairie**
- **Ener-G Foods**
- **Bob's Red Mill**
- **Koda Farm**

Best flours to substitute for sweet white rice flour:

None. We've had testers substitute regular white rice flour in our recipes with unfortunate results. The flours have a very different texture and flavor.

Sweet White Rice Flour Tips:

- In general, recipes with sweet white rice flour can get away with fewer binders. It's sticky on its own and will bind better than other flours. If your baked goods taste gummy, back off on the xanthan or guar gum.

- Sweet white rice flour likes to soak up liquid. You may find you need to use a little extra in your recipes.

- Sweet white rice flour can add a wonderful chewy texture to baked goods, as it does in our Cinnamon Rolls recipe.

- It does not provide much structure to baked goods on its own.

- It is not recommended for use with our vegan pancake and waffle recipes unless you're looking for something that tastes like mochi, a Japanese rice cake.

Fun uses for sweet white rice flour

- Mix with an equal amount of starch when making breading for frying meat
- Use to thicken white sauce

Chocolate Wafers

· ·

These cookies are a chocolaty take on the traditional Nilla Wafer! Use them as you would vanilla wafers to snack on, or crushed as the crust to your favorite cheesecake or pie.

Yield: Two large cookie sheets

DIRECTIONS:

1. Cream the butter, sugar and salt.

2. Add the vanilla extract and egg. Continue to beat.

3. Add in the remaining ingredients. Mix well. The dough will be thick.

4. Preheat oven to 330 degrees F.

5. Oil your hands. Roll teaspoon sized balls of dough. Press the dough into small medallions between the palms of your hands, similar to small sand dollars.

6. Place ½ inch apart on ungreased cookie sheet. This recipe will fill 2 large cookie sheets.

7. Bake 22-23 minutes. Rotate trays once during cooking time.

8. Remove from oven and allow the cookies to cool before removing them from the tray.

Store at room temperature or in the freezer for a later date.

INGREDIENTS:

9 tablespoons Earth Balance butter or shortening

¾ cup unrefined granulated sugar

¼ teaspoon salt

1 tablespoon pure vanilla extract

1 large egg

81 grams sweet rice flour (½ lightly filled cup + 3 tablespoons)

35 grams superfine rice flour (¼ lightly filled cup)

60 grams potato starch (⅓ cup)

50 grams cocoa powder (½ cup)

¾ teaspoon xanthan gum

Flaky Pie Crust

....

This recipe might just be the star of this book. It's been tested in nearly 30 kitchens. It behaves exactly like gluten-based pie crust and will remind you of the tasty crust that can be found in Marie Callender pot pies. We like to make this crust in the food processor though you may also make it by hand. With butter crusts you have to be careful not to overwork the dough as you will lose the flakiness. That is not the case here; it can be heavily worked and still yield gorgeous and delicious flakes.

Yield: Two pie crusts

Directions:

1. Combine all the dry Ingredients: sweet rice flour, rice flour, potato starch, salt, and xanthan gum in the bowl of a food processor.

2. Add the room temperature butter. Cut in by pulsing the machine until the butter is cut into small pea-sized pieces.

3. Add eggs and water. Process until it becomes thick dough. Dough should be soft and easy to work with- if needed add up to 1 additional tablespoon of cold water.

4. Roll dough out on a sheet of parchment paper, topping both the top and bottom with additional sweet rice flour as needed to prevent sticking.

5. Roll the parchment onto itself and then unroll into the pie plate.

6. Optional: brush with egg wash.

7. Bake at 375 degrees F 25-30 minutes until slightly golden.

Note: Be sure to roll out and place the dough into the pan promptly after making it. As it sits it will begin to dry out and become hard to work with. Keep dough covered. If the dough begins to dry out, knead in a little extra water, 1 teaspoon at a time. Eggs are the magic ingredient in this recipe; they make the flakiness possible. We strongly encourage that you do not attempt to make this recipe without them.

Recipe Variation: Make Poptart-Style Pastries like the ones on our cover. Roll out the dough and cut into the shape of your choice. Fill and sandwich two pieces of dough with your favorite fruit frilling. Jelly or jam will work best. Seal the edges of each pastry with a fork. Place on a cookie sheet and bake 25-30 minutes until golden. An egg wash is optional. Drizzle each pop tart with fruit or a frosting glaze.

Ingredients:

- 176 grams sweet rice flour (1½ lightly filled cups)
- 110 grams brown rice flour (¾ lightly filled cup)
- 52 grams potato starch (¼ cup + 1 tablespoon)
- 1 teaspoon salt
- ¼ teaspoon xanthan gum
- 14 tablespoons (1¾ stick) Earth Balance butter or shortening or bacon lard, room temperature
- 2 large eggs (cold or at room temperature)
- ¼ cup cold water

Egg Wash:

- 1 egg + 1 tablespoon water whisked together

Cinnamon Rolls with Espresso Icing

This recipe has brought tears of joy to many. We knew it was possible to re-create absolutely delicious rolls without the use of gluten. It was quite a task; nearly 30 trials went into this recipe's development. The end result is one we know your family and friends will devour, gluten-free or not. Using a kitchen scale and the exact ingredients specified below will yield the very best results.

Yield: One dozen cinnamon rolls

Directions:

1. Turn oven on to 350 degrees F. Once oven reaches this temperature, turn it off, being sure to keep the door shut.

2. Prepare a 9 x 9 inch square pan by drizzling 1 tablespoon of melted butter or oil and mixing in the 2 tablespoons of sugar. Coat the bottom of the pan.

3. In a small bowl, combine the lukewarm milk, sugar and yeast. Stir and set aside for 5-10 minutes.

4. In the bowl of a stand mixer, make the dough. Combine the rice flour, sweet rice flour, tapioca starch, potato starch, xanthan gum, baking powder, sugar, and salt.

5. Pour in the yeast/milk mixture, eggs and oil. Mix on high until the dough becomes very sticky (and begins to stick to the bowl).

6. Grease a large sheet of parchment paper. Using a spatula, plop the sticky glob of dough onto the center of the parchment.

7. Drizzle a little oil on the surface of the blob of dough and heavily oil your hands. Using your hands, press the dough into an 18 x 10 inch rectangular shape. Cover with the filling ingredients, starting with the butter or oil, then sugar and cinnamon.

Ingredients:

- 1 tablespoon melted butter or oil
- 2 tablespoons granulated sugar
- 272 grams lukewarm milk (1 cup + 3 tablespoons)
- 2 teaspoons of granulated sugar
- 11 grams fast-acting yeast (1 tablespoon)
- 200 grams superfine white rice flour (1½ lightly filled cups)
- 110 grams sweet rice flour (1 lightly filled cup)
- 130 grams tapioca starch (1¼ lightly filled cup)
- 28 grams potato starch (¼ lightly filled cup)
- 8 grams xanthan gum (2¼ teaspoons)
- 17 grams double acting baking powder (1 tablespoon)
- ⅓ cup granulated sugar (any variety except coconut palm or xylitol)
- 5 grams salt (½ teaspoon)
- 2 large eggs
- 50 grams melted butter or oil (4 tablespoons)
- ¼ cup melted butter or oil
- ¾ cup granulated sugar
- 1-2 tablespoons cinnamon

Espresso Icing:
- 1 cup powdered sugar
- ½ cup softened butter or shortening
- 3 tablespoons espresso
- 1 teaspoon vanilla extract
- Pinch of salt

8. Use the parchment paper as your guide to roll up the dough lengthwise.

9. Dust the surface of the rolled dough with a little sweet rice flour for easier slicing. Rotate the roll to sprinkle the flour on all sides. When finished placed the roll back to seam side down. Use a strand of dental floss to slice the dough into 12 rolls.

10. Place the cut rolls side by side in the prepared baking pan. Brush a tiny bit of melted butter or oil onto the top of each roll. Cover with a towel and place into the warmed oven for 25-30 minutes to rise.

11. After the 25-30 minutes, remove from oven, leaving the towel on pan. Turn on oven to 375 degrees F. Once fully preheated, place the rolls back in without the towel and bake for 16 minutes. Turn the oven down to 350 degrees F and bake an additional 8-10 minutes. Remove from the oven. Keep an eye on the rolls during the last 15 minutes of the cooking time; if they begin to get too brown, cover with a sheet of aluminum foil. Once you have removed the rolls from the oven, cover the pan again with the towel and allow to cool.

12. To make the glaze, combine all of the ingredients. Place prepared glaze on semi-cooled rolls.

Cutout Sugar Cookies

. . . .

Sugar cookies, with a little help from sweet rice flour, are easy to make. This dough will hold together, cut cleanly and bake to perfection. Bring them to all your holiday parties and watch as they disappear before the other cookies.

Yield: 4 trays

DIRECTIONS:

1. In a bowl, combine the rice flour, sweet rice flour, tapioca starch, and xanthan gum. Cut in the shortening until it is in pea-sized pieces.

2. Add the sugar, baking powder and salt. Stir in the eggs, vanilla extract and milk. The dough will be thick and not overly sticky.

3. Preheat oven to 350 degrees F. Lightly oil 2-3 large baking sheets.

4. Lightly dust a clean countertop with some sweet rice flour or rice flour. Roll the dough out ¼- ½ inch thick, dusting with more flour as needed to prevent sticking. Cut cookies using your favorite cookie cutters.

5. Place on the prepared baking sheet and bake 7-8 minutes.

6. Allow to cool before frosting.

Note: Xylitol is not recommended for this recipe; it gives the cookies a strange texture. If you like your cookies to be on the fluffier side, use ½ teaspoon of xanthan gum and only 2 teaspoons vanilla extract. If you prefer them a little denser, use the ¾ teaspoon xanthan gum and 1 tablespoon of vanilla extract as listed above.

INGREDIENTS:

210 grams white rice flour (1¼ packed cup)

148 grams sweet rice flour (1¼ lightly filled cup)

86 grams tapioca starch (¾ cup)

¾ teaspoon xanthan gum

153 grams shortening (1 cup)

310 grams organic white cane sugar (1½ cups)

1 teaspoon double acting baking powder

⅛ teaspoon salt

2 large eggs

1 tablespoon pure vanilla extract

59 grams milk (¼ cup)

Snickerdoodles

· ·

Enjoy these chewy cookies at your next holiday gathering—or anytime you want a sweet cinnamon treat. They freeze well so you can make a batch and then enjoy one a day. If you can stop at just one, that is.

Yield: Two dozen cookies

Directions:

1. Pour boiling water over flax seed meal in a small bowl. Stir and set aside for 10 minutes to gel.

2. In a large bowl, whisk together the sweet white rice flour, potato starch, cream of tartar, baking soda, cinnamon, and salt.

3. In a large bowl, cream together the shortening and maple syrup with a beater on medium speed.

4. Once 10 minutes have elapsed, beat the flax mix into the shortening then add the dry ingredients, continuing to beat until completely mixed. Cover and chill in the fridge for an hour.

5. Preheat the oven to 400 degrees F. Lightly oil or grease 2 cookie sheets. In a small bowl, stir together the sugar and cinnamon.

6. Remove dough from fridge and scoop into balls, approximately 2 tablespoons in size. Roll them in the cinnamon and sugar, then place on the cookie sheet and flatten. They puff up when baking, so you can flatten them quite a bit.

7. Bake for 10-11 minutes. Remove from oven and allow to cool for a few minutes before removing to a cooling rack.

Store in an airtight container at room temperature or freeze for later use.

Ingredients:

- 2 tablespoons ground flax seed meal
- 6 tablespoons boiling water
- 271 grams sweet white rice flour (1¾ lightly filled cups)
- 172 grams potato starch (1 cup)
- 2 teaspoons cream of tartar
- 1 teaspoon baking soda
- 1 teaspoon ground cinnamon
- ¼ teaspoon salt
- 1 cup shortening
- 1 cup maple syrup
- ¼ cup unrefined granulated sugar
- 1 teaspoon ground cinnamon

Nilla-Style Wafers

One egg is the secret to these spot-on copycat cookies. It, in combination with the butter and flour, makes for cookies with the perfect texture. Banana pudding anyone?

Yield: 2 large cookie sheets

Directions:

1. In the bowl of a stand mixer or using a hand mixer cream the butter, sugar, and salt.

2. Add the vanilla extract and egg. Continue to beat.

3. Add in the remaining ingredients. Mix well. The dough will be thick.

4. After this hour, preheat oven to 330 degrees F.

5. Oil your hands. Roll teaspoon sized balls of dough. Press the dough into small medallions between the palms of your hands so they resemble a small sand dollars.

6. Place ½ inch apart on an ungreased cookie sheet.

7. Bake 22-23 minutes, rotating trays once during cooking time.

8. Allow the cookies to cool before removing them from the tray.

Store at room temperature or in the freezer for a later date.

Ingredients:

9 tablespoons room temperature butter or shortening

¾ cup unrefined granulated sugar (cane sugar is recommended)

¼ teaspoon salt

1 tablespoon pure vanilla extract

1 large egg

100 grams sweet rice flour (½ packed cup + 2 tablespoons)

60 grams superfine rice flour (½ packed cup)

60 grams potato starch (⅓ cup)

¾ teaspoon xanthan or guar gum

Powdered Fried Cake Doughnuts

* *

Developing a fantastic gluten-free fried doughnut can be quite a challenge. During our testing process we learned that adding 1-2 tablespoons of oil to the recipe prevented the doughnuts from becoming too greasy. We also found that a fine-grained sugar performed the very best across the board.

Yield: One dozen doughnuts

DIRECTIONS:

1. Add oil several inches deep to a heavy bottomed sauce pan or deep fryer. Heat over medium-high heat while you prep the batter.

2. In a large bowl, mix the potato starch, sweet rice flour, superfine rice flour, xanthan gum, powdered sugar, baking powder, and salt.

3. Whisk in the milk, oil and egg. The batter will resemble thick cake batter.

4. Cut out several 3 x 3 inch squares of parchment paper. Coat them in a little oil.

5. Pour the donut batter into a piping bag fitted with the largest tip.

6. Pipe circular doughnut shapes onto each sheet of prepared parchment. Start small and work into a larger size as you get more comfortable.

7. Test your oil. It should be between 345-355 degrees F for best results. If you do not have a thermometer, adjust the heat after you test your first doughnut. The doughnut should grow 3-4 times its size when fried. It should slowly become golden brown over a period of about 2 minutes. Adjust the heat as needed to get those results.

8. Drop the first 3 x 3 inch square upside down into the oil. After a moment, take a pair of tongs and remove the parchment. The donut will begin to rapidly expand. Flip once or twice to cook on both sides.

9. Remove from the oil and place on a paper towel. Once semi-cooled, sprinkle with additional powdered sugar.

10. Continue with the remaining batter.

Notes: These doughnuts can also be baked. If you have a doughnut pan and would like to try baking half the batch, go for it! Oil the doughnut pan and pipe batter in. Bake at 360 degrees F for 15-20 minutes.

Donuts taste best if eaten within 24 hours. If not serving immediately, store the doughnuts at room temperature in a sealed bag.

INGREDIENTS:

Oil for deep frying

51 grams potato starch (¼ cup + 1 tablespoon)

36 grams sweet rice flour (¼ lightly filled cup)

65 grams superfine rice flour (½ lightly filled cup)

¼ teaspoon xanthan gum

94 grams powdered sugar (½ cup)*

1 ½ teaspoon double acting baking powder

½ teaspoon salt

½ cup milk

2 tablespoons oil

1 large egg

½ cup butter

¼ cup refined cane sugar

155 grams sweet white rice flour (1 lightly filled cup)

1 teaspoon pure vanilla extract

1 tablespoon cold water

2 large eggs

1 cup refined cane sugar

½ teaspoon baking powder

2 tablespoons fresh lemon juice

(Optional) powdered sugar or coconut flakes

Lemon Bars

These are a gluten-free version of an old family favorite from Dorothy R. Bates' Kids Can Cook. Even our friends who say they don't like lemon-flavored desserts go back for seconds on these. This recipe uses regular refined white sugar. We've tried it with unrefined sugars and the result is just not the same.

Yield: 16 squares

DIRECTIONS

1. Preheat oven to 350 degrees F. Grease an 8 x 8 inch baking dish.

2. Beat together the butter, sugar, sweet white rice flour, vanilla extract, and water. Press into the baking dish and bake for 20 minutes. Remove from oven.

3. Whisk the eggs, sugar, baking powder and lemon juice together. Pour evenly over the crust, then return to oven for 20 minutes.

4. Dust with powdered sugar or coconut flakes if desired. Let cool completely, and chill in the fridge before serving.

Store in an airtight container in the fridge.

Ask the Expert

Carol Fenster's books have delighted millions, and her book, *Gluten-Free Quick and Easy*, is a personal favorite of ours. She blogs at www.CarolFensterCooks.com and is a spokesperson for the United Sorghum Checkoff.

How long have you been baking gluten-free? I have been baking gluten-free since 1988, when I was told to avoid wheat by a holistic allergist who had the foresight to look beyond true allergies and test me for intolerances.

What flours do you find work best in place of rice flour? I rarely bake with white rice flour because it's too gritty, instead I use brown rice flour. I find that it exchanges nicely with sorghum flour on a 1:1 basis. I also use millet flour (1:1). And I really like to use buckwheat flour in place of rice flour (again 1:1), but regular buckwheat flour is too strongly flavored to be very versatile. So, instead of buying the flour, I use a spice grinder to grind up Bob's Red Mill Creamy Buckwheat Cereal into flour. Their cereal isn't toasted so it is much milder in flavor and works beautifully when used in place of sorghum or brown rice flour.

Have you noticed a difference in results between white and brown rice flour in baked goods? Definitely. White rice flour is much grittier than brown rice flour, so I much prefer the latter.

What flours besides rice do you find work well exchanged for each other? I often use potato starch and cornstarch interchangeably but know that cornstarch produces a crispier end product. So, if I want a crispier cookie I might add ¼ cup cornstarch to the batter (replacing same amount of flour blend) or better yet, design the cookie recipe with that in mind.

What are the top three things every new baker should know?

1. Read the recipe all the way through before starting so you can have everything ready, including the right ingredients and pans.

2. Follow the recipe exactly as written the first time you make it; then if you want to make substitutes make them the next time you bake.

3. Measure correctly and bake thoroughly. Improper measuring is the chief cause of baking flops while insufficient baking times usually cause falling, especially in cakes and breads.

Do you have any money saving tips for gluten-free bakers? Make your own flour blends to save money. However, adopt the baking style that fits you. If you prefer to buy a commercial flour blend, then experiment until you hit on one that you and your family like. Store gluten-free ingredients appropriately so they don't deteriorate. Save everything; even your bread flops can be pulverized in a food processor to make bread crumbs.

What are your favorite flours to work with and why?

1. Sorghum flour, because it has more protein and fiber than brown rice flour but is just as versatile. I think sorghum has the closest taste to wheat of all the gluten-free flours.

2. Sweet rice flour, because it brings an elasticity and pliability to baked goods like pie crusts that make them super-easy to roll out.

3. Expandex, which is really modified tapioca starch that makes our baked goods rise higher, have a more "normal" texture, and extends the shelf life. It has a totally neutral taste and is pure white so it doesn't affect the appearance of your baking. I use it in breads and muffins for a higher rise and in items that I want to be extra-crispy such as Graham Crackers.

What are your favorite types of recipes to bake and why?

1. Breads, especially yeast breads, because I missed bread the most when I went gluten-free.

2. Pizza, because I just love pizza.

3. Cakes, especially chocolate cakes, because I'm a chocoholic.

What kind of recipes would you suggest for a beginner to start with? Start with smaller-sized recipes that can be baked in small containers. Muffins are perfect. Most recipes make 12-muffins; standard muffins are (by definition) small. They don't have to rise a lot to be successful, the heat can get to all parts of the muffin because of the way the muffin pan is shaped so they cook evenly, and the shape of the pan also does the work for you by shaping the muffin as it bakes.

What's the most challenging recipe you ever developed and why? Flatbreads like naan and pita sound simple, but were actually a lot of work to get right. Choosing the flours and techniques to produce the desired effect took many, many tries.

Do you bake by weight or volume? When I develop recipes for manufacturers, I bake by weight, which is the most accurate way to do it whether I'm starting a recipe from scratch or modifying an existing one with a substitution. Unfortunately, most home cooks don't even have scales let alone know how to use them in baking so, thus far, my publishers haven't urged me to offer recipes using weight as well as volume. If we all baked by weight, there would be far fewer baking failures.

What do you generally use as egg replacers in baking? My usual egg replacements are ground flax seed and soft silken tofu, but I also use pureed fruit such as applesauce, pears or prunes. The pectin in fruits like applesauce, pears, and prunes is an excellent binder. I also use egg-replacer powder in recipes that have some other moisture because usually eggs contribute some of the leavening and some of the moisture in baking.

What kind of dairy-free replacements do you like to bake with? Do you think the changes affect the texture and flavor? I use the buttery spread by Earth Balance in place of butter, any kind of milk in place of cow's milk, and sour cream and cream cheese by either Tofutti or Follow Your Heart Vegan Gourmet. I'm also fond of yogurts by Whole-Soy and Wildwood.

Any replacement is bound to affect the texture and taste a bit, but our palates adjust as we go along to the point we come to accept the new version. For example, people who like the taste of cow's milk might initially dislike soy milk but as time goes on their palates come to prefer the taste of soy.

What differences have you noticed between tapioca starch, potato starch, and arrowroot starch? How do you decide which you want to use in a recipe? It depends on the recipe. While I might use potato starch and arrowroot interchangeably, I don't know of any other flour that performs just like tapioca so I am reluctant to replace it. It helps with browning of the exterior crust, plus it slightly crisps the outside of the crust and provides a little "chew" to the crumb. While you might not have recognized this, you will miss this crust in a cake or cookie that seems too soft on the outside and lacks the chew on the inside.

Can you give our readers some tips on how to get started with making bread without eggs? The replacement I use most is ground flax seed, preferably the golden variety if your bread is light-colored but all colors of flax seed perform the same. The ratios differ but basically I mix 1 to 3 tablespoons of ground flax seed with ½ to 1 cup boiling water and stir until well blended. Then let it sit for 5 minutes to thicken to a gel-like consistency that resembles raw egg whites. Use ¼ cup of this mixture for each large egg in baking. This works best for up to 2 eggs; recipes that call for more than that are so dependent on the egg's properties that the end result is likely to disappoint.

I have found that successfully baking without eggs is far harder than baking without wheat, so my best advice is to follow a recipe that has been designed to be egg-free rather than trying to figure it out on your own.

Is there anything else you think our readers should know about gluten-free baking? Follow the recipe and measure correctly. Make sure your oven is calibrated to bake at the right temperature. All ovens differ, but yours should be baking at the same temperature as indicated in the recipe, or you will most likely be under-or-over-baking your gluten-free items. Check yours with an oven thermometer that you can buy at the grocery store or a hardware store. The oven manual will explain how to calibrate it or have a service person do it for you.

Chapter 6

Potato Flour

· ·

First things first: potato flour is not potato starch. Potato starch is made from the isolated starch of raw potatoes and does not absorb much liquid until it is baked or cooked. Potato flour, on the other hand, is made from cooked potatoes (the peel and all) that are then dehydrated and ground. Potato flour absorbs large amounts of liquid. The two cannot be exchanged for one another.

Now that we got that out of the way, let's talk about how cool potato flour is. This funny flour is often ignored in gluten-free baking and we're not sure why. Once you understand it, you'll realize what a difference it can make in your baked goods. Adding potato flour will make your results chewier, and give you that extra spring you're missing from gluten. We started working on our bagel recipe very early in our development process for this book. We knew they had to have that unique chewy texture that makes a bagel, well, a bagel. It was easy for us to achieve the look of a bagel with other flours, but only potato flour was able to master the chewiness of traditional bagels.

Nutritional Highlights:

Potato flour is not high in nutritional value. Try combining it with a high-protein, high-fiber flour.

Brand Comparison:

The brands we tried were all equal in quality. The ones we tested were:

- **Dakota Prairie**
- **Bob's Red Mill**

Best flours to substitute for potato flour:

None. Even though it's used in small amounts in these recipes, it is absolutely integral.

Potato Flour Tips:

- Only use a small amount in recipes. Start with 1-2 tablespoons and increase if needed. The more you add, the more chew your baked good will gain.

- Potato flour absorbs liquid like crazy. When using it in recipes, add liquid a little at a time until you've reached the consistency you want.

- Best when used in savory recipes, as it lends a mild potato flavor.

- In our recipes, we noticed that as they cooled their texture changed. Initially out of the oven some recipes were gummy. However, at room temperature they became the texture we intended. Then when we chilled the baked good, it further changed and took on a harder texture. Warm up your baked goods for the best eating experience.

- Think of this flour like a French fry. When used in larger amounts it will give your baked goods a delicious crispy crust, while being soft on the inside. You will notice and love this quality in our Waffle Crisp Recipe.

Fun uses for potato flour

- Add a small amount (a few tablespoons) to cheese-free casseroles to add flavor.
- Flavorful way to thicken sauces

Mini Pizza Pockets

A crowd pleaser for kids and parents alike, these mini pizza pockets can be filled with your favorite toppings and frozen until you want to eat them. We like to make two batches at a time: one to eat right away, and a second batch to freeze.

Yield: Three dozen pockets

DIRECTIONS:

1. Preheat the oven to 350 degrees F. Take out 2 cookie sheets.

2. In a small bowl, stir together the flax seeds, psyllium husks, boiling water and olive oil. Let sit for 10 minutes.

3. In a large bowl, whisk together the potato starch, 44 grams (4 tablespoons) potato flour, salt, and oregano.

4. After the flax mixture has set, pour it into the dry ingredients, stirring until it's mixed together. Pour in the last 2 tablespoons of potato flour and knead it in until a ball forms. Place the dough on parchment paper and roll out as thin as possible. The thinner you roll it, the crispier they will be.

5. Cut out circles with a biscuit cutter. Place a small amount of pizza sauce, cheese and toppings in the center of each circle. Fold the circle in half, forming a crescent, and pinch the edges together.

6. Roll up the scraps and knead them back into a ball, roll out again, and continue the process until you've used up all your dough.

7. Once you have all your pizza pockets pinched into crescent shapes, brush both sides of each one with olive oil. Sprinkle with salt to taste.

8. Bake for 10 minutes. Remove from oven, turn over, and return to oven for another 10 minutes.

9. Let sit for 5 minutes. The filling will be very hot, so let it cool until the outside is just warm to the touch.

Note: You can freeze the pizza pockets after step 4. Put them in a container with parchment paper in between each layer. When ready to bake, simply take out of the freezer, brush with olive oil and bake as directed, adding an extra 3 minutes of baking time on each side.

INGREDIENTS:

- 1 tablespoon ground flax seed meal
- 1 tablespoon whole psyllium husks or ground chia seeds
- ¾ cup plus 2 tablespoons boiling water
- 1 tablespoon plus 2 teaspoons olive oil
- 86 grams potato starch (½ lightly filled cup)
- 66 grams potato flour (6 tablespoons)
- ½ teaspoon salt
- 1 teaspoon dried oregano
- Your favorite pizza sauce, cheese and toppings
- 2-4 tablespoons olive oil
- Salt to taste.

Naan

· ·

The year prior to going gluten-free my husband and I were bona fide Indian food junkies. At least twice a week we visited our favorite local restaurant and ate until we couldn't breathe. Now of course that isn't possible. This recipe is dedicated to my supportive husband who cheered me on as I worked endlessly to perfect this bread and bring our restaurant experience back home!

– Brittany

Yield: Four naan

Directions:

1. Turn on oven to 300 degrees F. Turn it off once it reaches the right temperature, keeping the door shut to create a proofing box.

2. Combine the warm water, yeast and sugar in a bowl. Stir and set aside to froth.

3. In a mixing bowl (the bowl of a stand mixer is ideal), combine the rice flour, potato starch, potato flour, xanthan gum, baking powder, and salt. Add the egg and the yeast mixture once it has begun to bubble and froth. Mix vigorously. The dough will be sticky.

4. Place a sheet of parchment on a cookie sheet. Lightly grease the parchment. Oil hands and divide the dough into 4 balls. Shape them into the traditional naan circular shape and place on the sheet. Each naan should be about ¼ inch thick. Brush oil on the top of each naan.

5. Cover tray with a towel and place into the warm oven for 25 minutes.

6. After the 25 minutes, remove tray from oven and turn the oven on to 450 degrees F. While the oven is preheating, brush the naan with oil or melted butter. Top with dried parsley, garlic and a dash of salt if you wish.

7. Place the tray of naan into the preheated oven and bake 12-15 minutes.

8. Let naan cool for 5 minutes and serve warm! This naan is slightly gummy when straight from the oven.

Note: Like all other rice-based gluten-free baked goods, the naan will lose its softness when it cools completely. Warm it up briefly before serving to soften again. You will be amazed how, even on the next day, a hard piece can become soft and fluffy with just a little time in the microwave.

Ingredients:

- 300 grams warm water (1¼ cup + 4 teaspoons)
- ½ tablespoon fast acting yeast
- 1 tablespoon granulated sugar (any variety except palm sugar or xylitol)
- 205 grams white rice flour (1¼ packed cup)
- 80 grams potato starch (½ cup)
- 25 grams potato flour (2 tablespoons)
- 1 teaspoon xanthan gum
- 2 teaspoons double acting baking powder
- ½ teaspoon salt
- 1 large egg

Paprika & Dill Waffle Crisps

We like to serve these crispy waffles at brunch as an alternative to hash browns. Try dipping them in ketchup or marinara sauce, and if you can have dairy, a dollop of sour cream.

Yield: Six squares

Directions:

1. In a large bowl, whisk together the brown rice flour, cornmeal, potato starch, potato flour, dill, paprika, and salt.

2. In a medium-sized bowl, whisk together the oil, water and milk.

3. Stir wet ingredients into dry until no longer lumpy.

4. Spoon evenly onto waffle iron and cook according to the iron's instructions. To make these crispy, check them when the iron says they're done. If the edges don't feel crispy, leave them in a few minutes longer. Serve hot.

Freeze leftovers. We found the best way to reheat them is to microwave until they're soft and then crisp them up by toasting them.

Ingredients:

32 grams brown rice flour (¼ lightly filled cup)

129 grams potato starch (¾ lightly filled cup)

70 grams cornmeal (½ cup)

44 grams potato flour (¼ lightly filled cup)

1 teaspoon dried dill

⅛ teaspoon smoked paprika

½ teaspoon salt

¼ cup mild flavored oil

2 cups water

½ cup unsweetened milk

Pita Bread

A call to all advanced bakers; this is the recipe
for you. Potato flour makes this recipe possible,
giving the bread the classic chewiness it should
have. Get out your kitchen scale and enjoy!

Yield: 5-6 rounds

DIRECTIONS:

1. In a cup, combine the warm water, yeast
   and granulated sugar. Stir briefly and set
   aside 5-10 minutes.

2. In the bowl of a stand mixer, combine the
   remaining Ingredients: rice flour, potato
   starch, potato flour, xanthan gum, baking
   powder, and salt.

3. Turn on oven to 300 degrees F. When it
   reaches 300 degrees F, turn it off and keep
   the door shut.

4. Once the yeast mixture has begun to foam, add it to the bowl of flour. Mix until the dough comes together and it is very sticky.

5. Place a sheet of parchment on a cookie sheet. Drizzle 1½ tablespoons of oil on the parchment. Use your hands to make sure the paper is fully covered.

6. Divide dough into 6 balls. Oil hands as needed to prevent sticking. Pat the dough into pita shaped disks making them ¼-½ inch thick. Place them side-by-side on the tray, leaving a little space in between them. Brush more oil on top of each round.

7. Cover with a towel and place into the warm oven. Let them proof in the oven for 20 minutes.

8. After 20 minutes, remove the tray from the oven and place it on top. Turn on oven and preheat it to 470 degrees F.

9. Once oven has reached 470 degrees F, remove the towel from the tray and quickly put the tray inside. Bake pita bread for 4 minutes. Open oven and, using a spatula, flip pitas on to their other side. Quickly close oven and let them bake an additional 6-8 minutes. It is during this second flip that the pitas will begin to puff up.

10. Remove from oven when they have begun to get some golden color. Allow them to cool 10-15 minutes before slicing. They are gummy when fresh out of the oven. The texture will change as they cool.

11. Cut in half.

Note: Pita bread is a finicky beast and in our experience all of the pitas in every batch don't always puff. We tested this recipe out with several brands of flour. We suggest for this recipe that you use only Bob's Red Mill white rice flour.

INGREDIENTS:

338 grams warm water

½ tablespoon fact acting yeast

½ tablespoon granulated sugar

200 grams Bob's Red Mill white rice flour

180 grams potato starch

12 grams potato flour

¾ teaspoon xanthan gum

1 teaspoon double acting baking powder

½ teaspoon salt

Bagels

··

Bagels are surprisingly easy to make. You'll notice this recipe contains a fourth flour; we found that sorghum gave the bagels the flavor and texture we were aiming for. Use a kitchen scale for the best results.

Yield: 4-6 bagels

DIRECTIONS:

1. Preheat oven to 350 degrees F then turn it off and keep the door shut to create a warm place for the bagels to rise.

2. Combine lukewarm water, sugar and yeast in a cup. Set aside to let the mixture froth and bubble for 5-8 minutes.

3. In a large bowl combine the rice flour, potato starch, sorghum flour, potato flour, xanthan gum, salt, and baking powder.

4. Stir in the eggs, yeasty water and oil. Using your hands, knead the dough until it comes together.

5. Line a cookie sheet with a piece of parchment paper. Lightly oil the parchment. Divide the dough into 4-6 balls, depending on how large you like your bagels.

6. One at a time, take each ball of dough between your hands and shape it into a clean ball. The cleaner the shape, the better your finished bagels will look. Any crevices will exaggerate when the dough rises.

7. Shape each ball of dough into a bagel. (Fun tip: We like to use a kitchen ring or English muffin ring to shape our bagels. We do this by placing the dough into the ring and using it as our guide. We place an oiled finger into the center of the dough and swirl it within the ring.) Make sure that your center hole is at least ½ inch wide as it will shrink when the bagels rise and bake.

8. Place the prepared bagels on the oiled parchment and cover with a towel. Place the pan into the warm oven. Allow the bagels to proof and rise for 25 minutes.

9. Meanwhile, bring a large pot of water to a boil on your stove.

INGREDIENTS:

- 210 grams (1 cup) warm water
- 1 tablespoon granulated sugar
- 1 tablespoon quick acting yeast
- 164 grams brown or white rice flour (1 packed cup)
- 110 grams potato starch (⅔ cup)
- 95 grams sorghum flour (¾ lightly filled cup)
- 24 grams potato flour (2 tablespoons)
- 14 grams xanthan gum (1 tablespoon)
- ½ teaspoon salt
- ¾ teaspoon double acting baking powder
- 2 large eggs
- 26 grams (3 tablespoons mild flavored oil)

EGG WASH:

- 1 egg whisked with 1 tablespoon water
- Your favorite bagel flavorings (coarse sea salt, poppyseeds, cinnamon, etc.)

10. After the 25 minutes of proofing, remove the bagels from the oven. Preheat oven to 375 degrees F.

11. While the oven is preheating, one at a time place each bagel into the boiling water for 20-25 seconds. After each bagel has been boiled, return it to the parchment-lined cookie sheet.

12. Brush the egg wash on each bagel. Top with coarse sea salt, poppyseeds or any of your other favorite toppings.

13. Bake the bagels for 25 minutes.

14. Remove from oven and allow to cool. As they cool they will gain their classic, chewy texture.

Once they have cooled, store these bagels sealed in a container or bag at room temperature or freeze for another day.

Try making Bagel Chips. Thinly slice bagels and place them on an oiled baking sheet. Drizzle each slice with additional oil and the spices of your choice. Bake at 325 degrees F until lightly browned. The chips will become crispy as they cool.

Ask the Expert

Peter and Kelli Bronski are the husband-and-wife-team behind the cookbooks, *Artisanal Gluten-Free Cupcakes* and *Artisanal Gluten-Free Cooking*. They are masters of bagel making and share fabulous recipes on their NoGlutenNoProblem blog. They are some of the only gluten-free bakers we know that use potato flour as often as we do. We're excited to share some of Peter's thoughts with you.

How long have you been baking gluten-free? I started baking GF in early 2007, after I was diagnosed with suspected celiac disease.

Do you remember the first thing you ever baked gluten-free (your recipe or someone else's)? How did it turn out? I sure do. It was a store-bought gluten-free pizza mix. I grew up on Long Island, NY, and my maternal grandfather is Sicilian so I feel like I had high pizza standards. But even so, this stuff was pretty horrid. The pizza "dough" had the consistency of heavy cake frosting before baking. We spread it in a pan, and when baked, it puffed to twice the height of a slice of Sicilian or Chicago-style deep-dish pizza. The texture was akin to sponge cake. The flavor was pretty unpalatable. Kelli couldn't finish her first slice. I couldn't finish my second. The rest of the pizza went in the garbage. That experience motivated us to do better by baking from scratch ourselves at home.

Do you ever use commercial gluten-free all-purpose mixes? If so, which brands do you prefer? If not, why not? In the very beginning we did. These days we almost exclusively use our own Artisan GF Flour Blend (the recipe is in our cookbooks and on our blog). But we do test other all-purpose GF flour mixes. For taste and texture, we've had good results with both blends that have higher percentages of whole grain flours, and ones that contain higher percentages of more refined GF starches. Nutritionally, we obviously prefer the whole grain versions. Whole grains are great for nutrition and the "wholesome" flavor, but having at least a little starch in an all-purpose blend improves texture, and often taste. Some blends offer the best of both worlds. We're pretty big fans of the GF Bistro all-purpose blend. As blends go, it's one of the best nutritionally, and when you learn how to bake with it, it yields great results. As a matter of personal preference, we tend to steer away from blends that are heavy on bean flours—we don't like their aftertaste, and sometimes their texture.

What are the top things every new baker should know? You may have a failure or two. Every baker does. Don't be discouraged. And don't throw out the flops! For example, if the bread doesn't turn out quite right, you can often still turn it into great GF bread crumbs, or make it into a French toast casserole.

Also, every new gluten-free baker needs to understand that you're baking without the thing that defines baked goods—gluten. It provides structure and elasticity in dough, and enables leavened breads and cakes (whether with yeast or baking soda/powder) to hold their risen shape. The more a recipe depends on that risen structure, in theory the harder it is to emulate. For example, pancakes are pretty standard whether GF or not. Breads and cakes and other such items get more tricky. It's all about mimicking the gluten protein, whether with xanthan gum, or egg whites, or ground flax. Use what works for you.

What tips would you give for someone wanting to convert a family favorite recipe to gluten-free? If you start with a good all-purpose GF flour blend, begin by doing a 1:1 swap for the wheat flour and see how things turn out. Based on the results, you can start to tweak from there. Or, do some benchmarking first. Search the Internet for other GF recipes similar to the family favorite you want to make, and see how others have made it, what quantities/ratios of ingredients they used, and which ingredients they chose. Then strategize from there.

How do you use potato flour in recipes? What texture and flavor do you think it imparts? What type of recipes do you use it in? We use potato flour as a component of our Artisan GF Flour Blend. The blend originally used tapioca starch, but because of the problem we encountered with variable flavors from brand to brand, some of which had an undesirable aftertaste, we "reformulated" our flour blend to eliminate the tapioca. In its place, we used potato starch with a small amount of potato flour. Varying the amount of potato flour made all the difference. By weight and by volume it doesn't make up much of our blend, but it yielded wonderfully moist baked goods with great crumb. And it's a more natural product, basically made from dehydrated whole potatoes, as opposed to potato starch made from the isolated starch.

What kind of recipes would you suggest for a beginner to start with? Don't start with a cherished family recipe, or one of your super favorite foods. It's just too risky because you have high expectations, and a very specific outcome in mind. If your gluten-free version doesn't measure up, you can get discouraged. Start with something simple that has a high success rate, such as pancakes, or pizza crusts.

Do you bake by weight or volume? When subbing one flour for another, do you do it by weight or volume? In the last six months or so we've switched to baking by weight—it's faster and more accurate. Once we made the switch, though, we were converts. When subbing flours, I think it's important to compare their textures first. If you're subbing fine flour for fine flour, or coarse for coarse, it won't matter as much which method you use. But if you have a lighter, coarser flour (say rice flour) and a finer flour (like potato flour), they'll weigh quite different for the same volume measure, and vice versa. The other thing to consider is how much moisture the respective flours will suck up. You may need to dial the substitution up or down depending on how it impacts the moisture of the dough or batter. It's complicated, and we don't have a standard method for substitutions.

What do you generally use as egg replacers in baking? If you use more than one, how do you decide which to use in a recipe? When replacing eggs, the most important thing to consider is why the eggs are in the recipe. If they provide moisture, then many replacements—applesauce, Ener-G—will work. But if the eggs provide structure from their protein, you want to go more with something like ground flax meal in warm water. Ener-G egg replacer is all carbs, no protein, so it's not a good choice if the eggs' protein is why they're in the recipe.

Chapter 7

Cassava Flour

· ·

Cassava flour is new to the gluten-free market. It's derived from the same plant as tapioca starch and while tapioca is primarily the starch of the plant, cassava flour makes use of the whole plant. The flour's infancy in the market did not enable us to do as much research and testing as we would have liked. We are grateful for the assistance of American Key Food Products, the manufacturer of cassava flour, for its contributions to this chapter. Food Scientist Carter Foss, the company's founder, and Chef Mark Hetzel provided the content below. Additionally, the recipes in this chapter have been provided by American Key Food Products and are not multi-allergen free. Use our recommended substitutions from Chapter 1 if needed.

Can you tell us a little bit about Cassava? What it is and how it is manufactured?

Premium Cassava Flour is derived from cassava roots. Cassava, also known as manioc, is a plant that grows in tropical climates close to the equator. The current conventional name for products derived from cassava is "tapioca". Thus, you may already be aware of tapioca flour, tapioca starch and tapioca pearls. These are all processed from cassava roots.

Cassava flour is manufactured by removing the outer layer of the whole root and following with a series of grinding, pressing, drying, and milling steps. Premium cassava flour is processed in a similar fashion. However, there are distinctive steps in the drying and the milling steps to ensure that the flour will conform to unique specifications that will optimize the flour for gluten-free baking applications. These unique specifications, as well as the manufacturing process, were specially developed by American Key Food Products and are the subject of a patent application.

What is the difference between Tapioca Starch and Cassava Flour?

The difference between our cassava flour and tapioca starch is essentially the same basic difference between other flours and their corresponding starches, such as potato flour and potato starch: all starches are manufactured using the optimum technologies to extract the most starch from the source, whether it is a grain or a tuber, which is the starch source. Flour manufacture does not use such processes. Most tapioca products come from Thailand. The leading Thai tapioca manufacturers offer a concise differentiation between the flour and the starch: tapioca starch is the flour without the fiber; tapioca flour is the starch with the fiber. The tapioca starch manufacturing process includes removing the pulp or fiber present in the roots. The flour manufacturing process does not include this step. Thus, the flour contains a significant amount of fiber not present in the starch product.

The two products are, however, similar: both the tapioca starch and the flour products have a high tapioca starch content, although the tapioca starch obviously is almost pure starch.

What kinds of recipes are best to make for first time cassava flour users?

Keep it simple; try brownies, cookies and muffins.

What characteristics does cassava flour attribute to baked goods?

1. Keeps baked goods moist
2. Good crumb texture
3. Pleasant flavor

Do bakers need to use xanthan or other gums when baking with cassava flour?

Yes and no. We have been successful formulating recipes such as cookies, brownies and cakes with no added gums. In recipes that call for a gum it is 25-50% less than we see in typical gluten-free recipes.

Would you categorize cassava flour as a pastry flour? Bread flour? Or an all-purpose flour?

Cassava would be along the lines of a cake or pastry flour. That's why it can be used by itself baking cookies or cakes. In the world of gluten-baked breads, there are no breads baked using cake flour. That's the same for the cassava flour. If you want to bake bread then you do need to help it with that addition of another starch or gum.

Does cassava flour impart any flavor to its baked goods?

It has a very subtle nuttiness to it, which shows nicely in pancakes, crepes and breads. Cassava flour lacks overpowering flavor notes that are sometimes apparent in other gluten-free flours.

How do baked goods hold up in the freezer using this flour?

The freeze-thaw capabilities of baked goods made with the cassava flour are impressive. If the home baker's practice is to regularly freeze baked goods, a little added xanthan can help with the problem of crumbling commonly seen with frozen goods. As with all baked goods, proper care in storing goods air-tight in the freezer and thawing them in the container will give the best results.

What is the best starting point for an individual wanting to try cassava flour?

Our experience is that placing it into a wheat-based recipe will be the quickest path to success. A good starting point is to begin at about 80-85% of the weight of wheat flour. If using it in a gluten-free-based recipe, substitute it at 10% of each flour/starch across the board in the recipe. For example, if a recipe has three flours in it, take 10% of each away and add that amount of cassava flour.

When will cassava need additional starches (tapioca, potato, etc.) in the recipe?

Additional flours/starches are needed for most bread formulations and that it may also be advantageous to add other flours/starches to achieve certain textural objectives. This is more a matter of individual preference than it is the ability of cassava flour to function as a single flour for gluten-free baking.

How does cassava react to liquid?

Cassava flour will generally require a slight adjustment in the liquid portion of a converted recipe due to its ability to absorb a greater amount of liquid than most gluten-free flours and some wheat based flours.

Can you list some of the benefits that come with including this flour in your baked goods?

1. Moisture retention

2. Ability to use as a single flour in a gluten-free recipe

3. Ability to be used without or with a low percentage of xanthan (or other gums) in many applications

4. Fiber and protein content

Can you give our readers some tips to help them get started?

1. Do not try to use it as a substitute for a blend of gluten-free flours/starches in a recipe. Begin to add it in small increments to see how it performs in the recipe.

2. It works best when converting from a wheat-based recipe.

3. It has a great synergy with rice flour and potato starch.

3. A small percent of Premium Cassava Flour added to your favorite bread recipe will help to add flavor and improve the texture of the crust.

Snickerdoodles

· ·

Yield: Three dozen

DIRECTIONS:

1. Preheat oven to 375 degrees F.

2. In a bowl sift flour, cream of tartar, salt, and baking powder together.

3. In a separate bowl, cream the shortening and sugar, scraping the bowl occasionally. Then add eggs and mix.

4. Slowly add flour mixture a little at a time and mix.

5. Cover and refrigerate dough for 2 hours.

6. Roll into balls the size of walnuts.

7. Roll into a mixture of sugar and cinnamon.

8. Place about 2 inches apart on ungreased cookie sheet. Bake 8 minutes. Cool on tray for 2 minutes before moving to rack.

INGREDIENTS:

2 cups Premium Cassava Flour

2 teaspoons cream of tartar

1 teaspoon baking soda

½ teaspoon salt

1 ½ cups sugar

½ cup shortening

½ cup butter

2 eggs

BLEND:

1 tablespoon sugar

1 teaspoon ground cinnamon

1 cup butter

1 cup + 1 tablespoon
Premium Cassava
Flour

2 cups granulated sugar

¾ cup cocoa powder

½ teaspoon salt

4 eggs

½ cup chocolate chips
(mini)

Brownies

· ·

Yield: Quarter Sheet

DIRECTIONS:

1. Preheat the oven to 350 degrees F. Melt the butter and set aside.

2. Blend the flour, sugar, cocoa powder, and salt. Add the eggs to the dry mix, then the butter.

3. Stir in the chips.

4. Spread onto a parchment lined sheet pan to desired thickness.

5. Bake for 20-30 minutes depending on your desired brownie texture preference.

Peanut Butter Cookies

Yield: Two dozen cookies

DIRECTIONS:

1. Mix flour, baking soda, baking powder, and salt in a bowl and set aside.

2. In a large bowl, mix sugars, and cream in the butter and shortening, scraping the bowl occasionally. Add the egg and peanut butter and mix. Stir in remaining ingredients. Cover and refrigerate about 2 hours.

3. Preheat oven to 375 degrees F. Shape dough into 1¼-inch balls. Place about 3 inches apart on ungreased cookie sheet. Flatten in crisscross pattern with fork dipped into sugar.

4. Bake 9 to 10 minutes or until light golden brown. Cool 2 minutes before moving to wire rack.

Variation: Add chocolate chips if desired.

INGREDIENTS:

1 cup Premium Cassava Flour

¾ teaspoon baking soda

½ teaspoon baking powder

¼ teaspoon salt

½ cup packed brown sugar

½ cup sugar

¼ cup butter

¼ cup shortening

1 egg

½ cup peanut butter

White Butter Cupcakes

INGREDIENTS:

1⅞ cups cassava flour

¼ teaspoon baking soda

2¼ cups sugar

1 cup (2 sticks) butter

6 eggs

1 cup sour cream

Yield: One dozen cupcakes

DIRECTIONS:

1. Sift the flour and baking soda together. Set aside.

2. Cream the butter and sugar until light, about 10-15 minutes scraping the bowl occasionally.

3. Add the eggs one at a time, scraping between additions. The closer in temperature the eggs are to the butter mixture the better the results will be.

4. Add in   of the dry ingredients just to blend. Add the sour cream, scrape well. Then add the remainder of the dry ingredients. Mix until thoroughly blended.

5. Place the batter into 12 greased cupcake tins and bake at 340-350 degrees F 20-25 minutes.

Chapter 8

Make Your Own Vegan Pancakes & Waffles

· ·

Everyone deserves to eat pancakes and waffles on Sunday morning. With this guide, you'll be able to choose your favorite flours, sweetener and spices, and make it your own. We made more than two dozen batches of pancakes to get this right, and we're confident that you won't go wrong with our tips and tricks!

INGREDIENTS:

1¼ cups or 158 grams flour (or mix of flours)

½ cup or 86 grams starch (potato starch is best)

2 teaspoons baking powder

½ teaspoon sea salt

2 tablespoons granulated sugar

¼ cup unsweetened applesauce

2 tablespoons mild flavored oil

½ to 1¾ cups water, milk or juice

Vegan Pancakes & Waffles

DIRECTIONS:
1. Whisk together your dry ingredients.

2. Whisk together the applesauce, oil and ½ cup of liquid. Pour the dry ingredients into the wet and stir. Add more liquid slowly until you've reached the consistency of a thick pancake batter. Always start with less liquid and test the batter on one pancake or waffle first. If it's too thick, you can add more liquid, but you can't take liquid away once you've added it!

- To make waffles, make sure to oil the iron frequently and keep the batter thick. It won't spread on the iron, but you can use a spoon to spread the batter out evenly on the iron. If the batter is too thin, it's much more likely to stick.

- To make pancakes, you can use a little more liquid than with waffles (about 2-4 tablespoons more), depending on how thick you prefer your pancakes.

Tips (Read These Before Making):

Best Flours/Starches to Use:
1. Potato starch is the best starch to use in these recipes. You can use tapioca, arrowroot, or cornstarch, but potato starch makes the insides fluffier.

2. Almond flour makes the best pancakes, hands down! They taste buttery and sweet. The batter should be equally thick for pancakes or waffles. However, this recipe does not work with only almond flour. Use the starch and you'll get amazing pancakes. If you try using just almond

flour without starch, your pancakes will be horrible excuses for pancakes that will make a mess of your pan. If you can eat almonds, we highly recommend you make this your go-to pancake mix.

3. Millet flour pancakes taste somewhat like biscuits, and are our second favorite flour to use. A mix of millet flour, almond flour and potato starch makes a heavenly pancake!

4. We love the flavor of buckwheat and teff. For a hearty mix, try either one or both.

5. Quinoa, sorghum and garbanzo bean flour all make fluffy pancakes and waffles. The flavors aren't our personal favorites, but they can be jazzed up with the addition of other flavors.

6. If using an all-purpose mix like Bob's Red Mill, skip the starch and use 1¾ cups of mix or 244 grams. Avoid mixes with xanthan or guar gum in them.

Flours to Avoid:

1. Brown rice flour makes a decent pancake, but it won't be as fluffy as the other flours and the flavor is somewhat bland.

2. This recipe does not work with coconut flour or cassava. To make coconut flour pancakes, see our Peanut Butter Pancake recipe in the coconut flour chapter in part 1 of our guide. You can, however, add 1-2 tablespoons of coconut flour to your flour

in this recipe. You'll have to increase your liquid if you do this.

3. Sweet white rice flour, amaranth flour, and white rice flour all tended to be a little gummy inside, so I wouldn't recommend using these. Brown rice flour had a nice texture and was good for a basic mix, although a bit bland for my liking.

Vary The Flavor:

1. For the sweetener, you can use 2 tablespoons of any granulated sugar. Coconut palm sugar, date sugar, and maple sugar all impart unique flavors to your pancakes. Alternatively, you can use 2 tablespoons of a liquid sweetener. Just add it to the wet ingredients instead. I personally thought the granulated sugar gave the best texture to the pancakes though.

2. For the applesauce, you can try using any puree. Banana, sweet potatoes and pumpkin work well. Applesauce makes a slightly fluffier pancake than some of the other purees.

3. Replace the oil with melted butter, coconut oil or margarine for a richer flavor.

4. You can use water, milk or juice as the liquid in this recipe. If you use full-fat canned coconut milk, you'll need more liquid than if you use water or milk. No matter the liquid or flours used, start with just ½ cup of liquid and increase as needed.

Chapter 9

Frostings

· ·

2 cups raw cashews, soaked in water 4 hours to overnight

4 dates

½-1 cup full-fat canned coconut milk

¼ cup maple syrup

¼ cup chopped fresh fruit (bananas, blueberries, strawberries, cherries, etc.)

Whipped Cashew Cream

This is a thick frosting, perfect for muffins, hearty cakes, or can even be used as a spread on quick breads.

Yield: 4 cups

DIRECTIONS:

Rinse and drain the cashews. Place in a food processor along with the rest of the ingredients. Start with just ½ cup of coconut milk. Process a few minutes, until completely smooth. Add up to ½ cup more coconut milk if a thinner consistency is desired.

Caramel Cream Frosting

· ·

You can adjust this recipe by using more or less powdered sugar. With less, the texture will be closer to a spread that you can use to dip fruit in. If you continue to add powdered sugar, the texture will change to that of a frosting.

Yield: One cup

DIRECTIONS:

1. Start by making your powdered sugar. Place the coconut palm sugar and starch in your blender. Make sure the blender is completely dry inside first. Blend the sugar and starch until it's the consistency of powdered sugar. Once it's ready, set it aside.

2. Rinse and drain the cashews, and puree them in a food processor with the lemon juice, vanilla extract, and salt. Continue to process them until the mixture is a thick, smooth consistency, scraping down the sides as necessary.

3. Add the shortening and process, then add the powdered sugar a little at a time, until you've reached the consistency you like. If a thicker consistency is desired, make more powdered sugar and add slowly.

INGREDIENTS:

- 1 cup coconut palm sugar (or more as needed)
- 2 tablespoons tapioca starch or arrowroot starch
- 1 cup raw cashews, soaked in water 4 hours to overnight
- 1 teaspoon lemon juice
- ½ teaspoon pure vanilla extract
- ¼ teaspoon salt
- 4 tablespoons shortening

1½ cups fresh berries (or frozen and thawed)

1 tablespoon fresh orange juice

20 drops liquid stevia

Berry Syrup

. . . .

This is the only recipe in this book using stevia. Although stevia has a bitter aftertaste, it is masked by the sweet berries. Use this as a syrup for your pancakes and waffles or try it drizzled over the Gingerbread Angel Food Cake.

Yield: ¾ cup

DIRECTIONS:

Puree all ingredients in a food processor or blender until smooth. If you're using a berry with large seeds, like raspberries, you can strain the sauce if you prefer not to have them in the syrup.

Homemade Powdered Sugar

INGREDIENTS:

⅓ cup any variety of granulated sugar

teaspoon arrowroot, cornstarch, tapioca, or potato starch

All varieties of granulated sugar can become powdered with the use of a blender or coffee grinder. Store bought powdered sugar usually contains cornstarch, which is problematic for some people. For those looking to avoid starch, it can be left out in most cases as its purpose is to help thicken frostings.

Try making powdered sugar out of organic cane sugar, coconut palm sugar, Sucanat, turbinado sugar, or xylitol. Each will provide a different flavor, level of sweetness and may change the color of your frosting slightly. Experiment to find which sugar you like working with best.

DIRECTIONS:

1. Process ingredients in a blender or coffee grinder until light and powdered. Store in an airtight container.

5 tablespoons cold water

1 packet unflavored gelatin

1 cup liquid sweetener (brown rice syrup, agave nectar, coconut nectar, or maple syrup)

Pinch of salt

Marshmallow Creme

Our take is a little healthier and surprisingly easy to make. The different sugars listed as options will create varying levels of sweetness. Select your favorite that best suits your dietary needs.

DIRECTIONS:

1. In a small microwave safe bowl, combine the cold water and gelatin. Microwave for 30 seconds.

2. In a large bowl, combine the gelatin and sugar. Whip vigorously using a mixer 8-10 minutes until it becomes thick. As it sits, it may begin to lose its fluffy appearance and curdle. If this happens you can re-beat with a spoon or spatula briefly. This marshmallow creme will get firm if stored in the fridge.

Note: If you want to keep things extra simple, use Suzanne's Ricemallow Creme, which can be found in many grocery stores.

Dairy-Free Buttercream

INGREDIENTS:

2½-3 cups powdered sugar (see powdered sugar recipe)

1 cup (2 sticks) Earth Balance Buttery Sticks or Spread

Earth Balance Buttery Sticks make flawless buttercream! For those who avoid soy, use their soy-free tub of butter instead. Use this recipe to frost your favorite cake or use a dollop on cookies. This frosting will hold its shape at room temperature.

Note: the amount of powdered sugar needed will range depending on what type of sugar you use. This is especially true when you opt to use our homemade powdered sugar recipe.

DIRECTIONS:

1. Combine softened Earth Balance butter and powdered sugar with a hand mixer.

2. Add more sugar for a thicker frosting; add more Earth Balance butter to thin it out.

Experiment with this frosting to customize the flavor for different applications. Some ideas to get you started:

- **Vanilla:** Add some pure vanilla extract and or fresh vanilla beans.
- **Mint:** Add fresh pureed mint leaves or mint extract.
- **Chocolate Almond:** Add cocoa powder to taste and almond extract.
- **Lemonade:** Add 1-2 tablespoons of condensed lemonade and lemon zest
- **Chai:** Start with ½ teaspoon each of ground cardamom and nutmeg (adding more to taste). Add a dash of pure vanilla extract.
- **Citrus Ginger:** Add 1 teaspoon grated ginger and 1 teaspoon orange or lemon extract.

1 can full-fat coconut milk (Thai Kitchen brand works best), chilled for at least a few hours

2½ cups coconut flakes (not reduced fat)

¼-½ teaspoon salt to taste

1½-2 tablespoons lemon juice

Liquid sugar to taste (agave nectar, maple syrup, coconut nectar, honey, or liquid stevia to taste)

Basic Coconut Cream Cheese

Dairy-free cream cheese alternatives tend to be comprised of either soy or nuts. We created this version without those two ingredients, as we know that many of you are not able to consume them. This thick cream cheese tastes best at room temperature. If it becomes hard and dry after storing in the fridge, stick it in the microwave 15-20 seconds to soften.

DIRECTIONS:

1. Place can of coconut milk in the fridge for a few hours to chill. This will allow the coconut cream to rise to the top.

2. Using a coffee grinder or powerful blender, make "coconut butter" by processing the coconut flakes until they becomes thick and smooth like peanut butter. You may need to stir the flakes several times until they are fully processed.

3. Place the thick coconut butter in a bowl. Remove can of coconut milk from the fridge and scoop out the thick portion of the heavy coconut cream, which will have risen to the top. Stir it into the coconut butter.

4. Stir in the lemon juice, salt and sugar. Give a taste test and adjust flavoring to taste.

Note: Try adding vanilla or other flavored extracts to this cream cheese. If you would like it thicker, add more "coconut butter". If you would like it thinner, add more coconut milk or liquid sugar.

Coconut Cream Cheese Frosting

....

So close to the real thing, no one will guess it's made without dairy, soy or nuts.

DIRECTIONS:

1. Using a coffee grinder or powerful blender make "coconut butter" by processing the coconut flakes until they become thick and smooth like peanut butter. You may need to stir the flakes several times until they are fully processed.

2. In a microwave safe bowl, add the coconut butter. Open can of chilled coconut milk and scoop out the heavy cream on top. Mix together and stir in the salt, sugar and lemon juice.

3. Melt mixture in the microwave for 30 seconds to 1 minute. Place in the fridge until thick and chilled.

4. Using a hand mixer, beat in xanthan gum. Start with ⅛ teaspoon, adding only up to ¼ teaspoon total if you want it thicker. Be careful not to add more than this as the frosting can become gummy.

This frosting stores great in the fridge. Use it to top cake or cookies.

INGREDIENTS:

1 cup coconut flakes (not reduced fat)

1 chilled can of full-fat coconut milk (Thai Kitchen brand is best)

¼ teaspoon salt

½ cup powdered sugar (see powdered sugar recipe)

1½ teaspoons lemon juice

⅛-¼ teaspoon xanthan or guar gum

1 ¼ cups unsweetened coconut flakes

¼-½ cup powdered sugar (see powdered sugar recipe)

¾ cup strawberries, pureed

1-1½ tablespoons lemon juice

½ teaspoon pure vanilla extract

⅛ teaspoon salt

Coconut Strawberry Cream Cheese

This healthy cream cheese recipe is perfect topped on cake, cupcakes, cookies or a bagel. You'll be surprised how many great uses it has. For variation, try subbing in different varieties of pureed fruit.

Yield: ½ cup

DIRECTIONS:

1. Using a coffee grinder, process the coconut flakes into butter. You may need to stir them several times before they process fully.

2. Next, make your own powdered sugar (or just use store bought). I recommend using a mild tasting sugar like cane or turbinado. Coconut palm sugar has a caramel flavor that may not work best in this application. Xylitol is not recommended.

3. Puree fresh or thawed frozen strawberries.

4. Combine the coconut butter, powdered sugar, strawberry puree, lemon juice, vanilla, and salt. Mix together (this can be done by hand or in a small food processor). At this point, give it a taste test and adjust the ingredients to taste. Store in the fridge.

Note: If you want the cream cheese thicker, add a pinch (keep it less than ⅛ teaspoon) of xanthan or guar gum or add as many additional coconut flakes ground into "butter" as you want.

Chocolate Glaze

• •

We love using this glaze with our Apricot Brownie Bites, but it can also be drizzled over cookies or cakes. Make sure your ingredients are at room temperature before you start. If not, the glaze will not become as uniformly smooth.

DIRECTIONS:

1. Heat coconut milk in a small pan over low heat. Stir in maple syrup and vanilla extract for a minute.

2. Add chocolate and stir until smooth.

You can dip your baked goods in this glaze and let them cool on parchment paper. Alternatively, you can drizzle the glaze over cookies and cakes.

INGREDIENTS:

(at room temperature)

½ cup full-fat canned coconut milk

6 tablespoons maple syrup

1 teaspoon pure vanilla extract

4 ounces unsweetened chocolate, chopped

3 dried apricots, finely chopped

¼ cup nut or seed butter

½ stick (4 tablespoons) Earth Balance or butter

2-2½ cups powdered sugar (see powdered sugar recipe)

3 tablespoons milk

Nut or Seed Butter Frosting

Cashew, peanut and sunflower seed butters are our favorites. Different brands of nut butter contain different levels of oil so you may need to adjust this recipe slightly adding more or less powdered sugar and milk to find the results that you like best.

DIRECTIONS:

1. Bring ingredients to room temperature. Combine using a hand mixer. If the frosting beads up, add additional milk ½ teaspoon at a time.

2. Cover and place frosting in fridge until its ready to be used. Try piping this frosting onto jelly-filled cupcakes!

German Chocolate Cake Frosting

* *

This thick frosting is delicious sandwiched between two cookies or spread over a German Chocolate Cake!

DIRECTIONS:

1. Select a base frosting such as Buttercream, Coconut Cream Cheese, or Whipped Cashew Cream.

2. If choosing the Coconut Cream Cheese, omit the lemon juice called for. If choosing the Whipped Cashew Cream, omit the fruit called for.

3. Add vanilla, coconut flakes and nuts.

INGREDIENTS:

1 teaspoon pure vanilla extract

½ cup unsweetened coconut flakes (or more to taste)

½ cup chopped pecans or walnuts (or more to taste)

Simple Soft Caramel

INGREDIENTS:

¾ cup butter, Earth Balance or coconut oil

1¼ cups brown sugar

¼ cup liquid sugar (corn syrup, agave nectar, brown rice syrup, coconut nectar, or honey)

6 ounces canned coconut milk

½ teaspoon salt

1 teaspoon pure vanilla extract

Our caramel is healthier than the pre-wrapped cubes that you'll find in the candy section of most grocery stores. Pull out your candy thermometer for this one.

DIRECTIONS:

1. In a large heavy-bottomed sauce pan, one large enough to allow for this mixture to expand without overflowing, Combine the butter, granulated and liquid sugar, coconut milk, and salt.

2. Using a candy thermometer, heat the mixture to 248 degrees (firm ball stage). Quickly stir in the vanilla.

3. Pour into a parchment lined 7 x 7 inch square pan, set aside, and allow to cool for several hours until firm. Caramel may also be spooned over cookies, or other favorite desserts while it is still warm. This caramel may be reheated and melted for future use.

Resources

Looking for more resources for baking tips and ideas? These are our favorite resources. Some of our ideas have come from cookbooks that aren't gluten-free, so we're including any references that we've found helpful. Check out some of these websites and books. Enjoy!

Books:

Artisanal Gluten-Free Cupcakes by Kelli and Peter Bronski

Beyond the Moon Cookbook by Ginny Callan

Cooking for Isaiah: Gluten-Free and Dairy-Free Recipes for Easy, Delicious Meals by Silvana Nardone

Everyday Raw Desserts by Mathew Kenney

Gluten-Free Baking for Dummies by Dr. Jean McFadden Layton and Linda Larsen

Gluten-Free Makeovers by Beth Hillson

Gluten-Free on a Shoestring by Nicole Hunn

Gluten-Free Quick & Easy by Carol Fenster

Go Dairy Free by Alisa Marie Fleming

Good Morning: Breakfasts without Gluten, Sugar, Eggs or Dairy by Ricki Heller

How Baking Works by Paula Figoni

Kids Can Cook by Dorothy R. Bates

The Flavor Bible: The Essential Guide to Culinary Creativity, Based on the Wisdom of America's Most Imaginative Chefs by Karen Page and Andrew Dornenburg

The Gluten-Free Almond Flour Cookbook by Elana Amsterdam

The Gluten-Free Gourmet: Living Well Without Wheat by Bette Hagman

The Spunky Coconut Cookbook by Kelly Brozyna

Magazines:

Gluten-Free Living
www.glutenfreeliving.com

Easy Eats
www.easyeats.com

Living Without
www.livingwithout.com

Fine Cooking
www.finecooking.com

Blogs and Websites:

Adventures of a Gluten-Free Mom
www.adventuresofaglutenfreemom.com

Affairs of Living
www.affairsofliving.com

Book of Yum
www.bookofyum.com/blog

Celiac Teen
www.celiacteen.com

Chocolate Covered Katie
www.chocolatecoveredkatie.com

Choosing Raw
www.choosingraw.com

Cook it Allergy Free
www.cookitallergyfree.com

Diet, Dessert, and Dogs
www.dietdessertndogs.com

Elana's Pantry
www.elanaspantry.com

Ginger Lemon Girl
www.gingerlemongirl.blogspot.com

Gluten-Free Easily
www.glutenfreeeasily.com

Gluten-Free Gigi
www.glutenfreegigi.com

Gluten-Free Goddess
www.glutenfreegoddess.blogspot.com

Gluten-Free on a Shoestring
www.glutenfreeonashoestring.com

Jenn Cuisine
www.jenncuisine.com

Karina's Kitchen
www.glutenfreegoddess.blogspot.com

Pure 2 Raw
www.pure2raw.com

Manifest Vegan
www.manifestvegan.com

She Let Them Eat Cake
www.sheletthemeatcake.com

Silvana's Kitchen
www.silvanaskitchen.com

Simply Sugar & Gluten-Free
www.simplysugarandglutenfree.com

Simply…Gluten-Free
www.simplygluten-free.com

Straight into Bed Cakefree and Dried
www.milkforthemorningcake.blogspot.com

Tasty Eats at Home
www.tastyeatsathome.com

The W.H.O.L.E. Gang
www.thewholegang.org

Whole Life Nutrition Kitchen
www.nourishingmeals.com

The Balanced Platter
www.balancedplatter.com

The Mommy Bowl
www.themommybowl.com

The Spunky Coconut
www.thespunkycoconut.com

Z's Cup of Tea
www.zscupoftea.com

Recipe Index

About the Authors

Brittany Angell, author of *The Essential Gluten Free Baking Guides, Parts 1 & 2,* is founder of the fast growing allergy-free food blog RealSustenance.com. At Real Sustenance, Brittany has created over 300 diverse and delicious recipes that are primarily gluten- & dairy- free. However, she strives to serve the entire allergy-free consumer by developing creative, unique and hard to find recipes that are also soy, egg, corn, sugar and grain free.

As a worldwide leader in food allergy awareness, Brittany is a sought-after author, speaker and consultant to corporations and restaurants seeking to capitalize on the expanding gluten- and allergy- free market.

Brittany's foray into the food allergy world began in January 2010 after many months of unsuccessfully solving her health issues through traditional means. Once she took her health into her own hands through education and research, she was led to several specialists and was diagnosed with Hashimoto's disease, along with various food allergies and intolerances. Her ultimate goal is to connect, engage and understand the needs of others and to guide them through their journey to health through education, support and recipe development.

Brittany resides in Rochester, NY with her husband and two rescued rat terriers.

Spankey Aguirre Photography

Iris Higgins is the author of TheDailyDietribe. com, a popular blog where she shares gluten-free recipes and her experiences with food and life. She focuses on using healthy ingredients to make dishes that everyone will love. Her first two cookbooks, with co-author Brittany Angell, take the mystery out of gluten-free baking. *The Essential Gluten Free Baking Guides* include over 100 gluten, dairy, and soy free recipes, as well as hundreds of tips for both new and experienced gluten-free bakers.

Iris has a master's degree in psychology from New York University, and is currently working on a second master's degree in nutrition from Bastyr University. In addition to writing her blog, Iris divides her time between school and individual weight-loss counseling with her clients. She lives in Seattle, Washington.